Lingua Latina A2
Latin – English
Interlinear Short Myths

Latin A2 Reade

Brian Smith

ISBN:9798227057662

De Creatione Mundi

In principio, Chaos erat. In hoc chaotico statu, omnia confusa et sine ordine erant. Nihil erat nisi infinita confusio. Tenebrae et vacuitas omnem locum complebant.

In the beginning, there was Chaos. In this chaotic state, all things were confused and without order. There was nothing but infinite confusion. Darkness and emptiness filled every space.

Ex hoc primigenio Chaos, mundus pulcher formatus est. Deus, magnus mundi creator, inchoavit ordinare Chaos et creare ex illo universum mirabile.

From this primordial Chaos, a beautiful world was formed. God, the great creator of the world, began to organize Chaos and create from it a marvelous universe.

Primo, Deus magnam divisionem fecit: terra a mari separata est. Terra firma emergit, ubi arbores altae et montes imponentes crescunt, et ubi animalia diversa habitant. Mare magnum est, profundum et vastum, ubi pisces innumerabiles et creaturae marinae natant, mundum aquaticum mirum et diversum efficiunt.

First, God made a great division: the land was separated from the sea. The solid earth emerged, where tall trees and imposing mountains grow, and where various animals live. The great sea is deep and vast, where countless fish and marine creatures swim, creating a wondrous and diverse aquatic world.

Caelum etiam, vastum et infinitum, creatum est. In caelo, Deus nubes et ventos posuit. Caelum, diurnum et nocturnum, caeruleum et stellatum, domus est avibus quae in aere volant et cursum siderum et planetarum.

The sky, too, vast and infinite, was created. In the sky, God placed clouds and winds. The sky, both by day and by night, blue and starry, is the home of birds that fly through the air and of the course of stars and planets.

Postea, ordo diei et noctis constitutus est. Die, sol magnificus in caelo lucet, calorem et lucem praebens. Nocte, luna argentata et stellae innumerabiles in caelo nitent, pulchritudinem nocturnam et mysterium profundum caeli monstrantes.

Then, the order of day and night was established. By day, the magnificent sun shines in the sky, providing warmth and light. By night, the silver moon and countless stars shine in the sky, revealing the beauty of the night and the profound mystery of the heavens.

Deinde, Deus aves in aere, pisces in aqua, et animalia in terra creavit. Aves variae species et colores habent et in caelo libere volant. Pisces, colorati et mirabiles, sub undis natant. Animalia in terra vagantur, multa et varia, magna et parva, lenta et celeria. Deus unicuique animali naturam et instinctum proprium dedit, ut in mundo suo unice vivat et floreat.

Next, God created birds in the air, fish in the water, and animals on the land. The birds have various species and colors and fly freely in the sky. The fish, colorful and wondrous, swim beneath the waves. The animals roam the land, many and varied, large and small, slow and fast. God gave each animal its own nature and instinct, so that it may live uniquely and thrive in its world.

In terra, Deus etiam herbas, flores et arbores creavit. Herbae et flores varii, pulchri et fragrantes, terram ornaverunt. Arbores, altae et robustae, vitam et umbram dabant. Fructus et semina ex his arboribus et plantis emergunt, alimentum praebentes multis creaturis.

On the land, God also created grasses, flowers, and trees. Various grasses and flowers, beautiful and fragrant, adorned the earth. The trees, tall and strong, provided life and shade. Fruits and seeds emerged from these trees and plants, providing nourishment for many creatures.

Tandem, Deus universum admirabile et ordinatum constituit, leges naturales statuens quae mundum regunt. Haec omnia Deus bona et pulchra esse vidit.

Finally, God established an admirable and orderly universe, setting natural laws that govern the world. God saw that all these things were good and beautiful.

Et sic mundus, cum hominibus, deis et natura, plenus factus est. Hoc est finis capituli de mundi creatione secundum Ovidii "Metamorphoses."

And thus the world, with humans, gods, and nature, became full. This is the end of the chapter on the creation of the world according to Ovid's "Metamorphoses."

De Apolline et Daphne

In antiqua Graecia, deus Apollo, clarus pro sua pulchritudine et sapientia, in silva ambulabat.

In ancient Greece, the god Apollo, famous for his beauty and wisdom, was walking in the forest.

Die illo, sol lucidus erat et aves canebant. Apollo, qui etiam deus musicae erat, citharam suam pulchre sonabat.

On that day, the sun was bright and the birds were singing. Apollo, who was also the god of music, was beautifully playing his lyre.

Dum Apollo ambulat, Cupido, deus amoris, apparet. "Salve, Apollo!" Cupido dicit. "Cur non amas? Ego sum deus amoris et volo te in amore esse."

As Apollo walked, Cupid, the god of love, appeared. "Greetings, Apollo!" Cupid said. "Why do you not love? I am the god of love and I want you to be in love."

Apollo ridet et respondet, "O Cupido, ego sum deus sapiens et fortis. Amor me non tangit."

Apollo laughed and replied, "O Cupid, I am a wise and strong god. Love does not touch me."

Cupido, iratus ob verba Apollinis, duas sagittas capit: unam auream, quae amorem facit, et alteram plumbeam, quae amorem repellit. Cupido Apollinem sagitta aurea tangit et Daphnen, nympham pulchram, sagitta plumbea.

Cupid, angry at Apollo's words, took two arrows: one golden, which creates love, and another leaden, which repels love. Cupid struck Apollo with the golden arrow and Daphne, a beautiful nymph, with the leaden arrow.

Apollo, statim amore Daphnes ardens, eam sequitur. "Daphne!" clamat. "Cur fugis? Ego sum Apollo, deus solis et musicae."

Apollo, immediately burning with love for Daphne, pursued her. "Daphne!" he called. "Why do you flee? I am Apollo, god of the sun and music."

Daphne, territa, fugere incipit. "Auxilium! Auxilium!" clamat. "Pater mi, Penee, adiuva me!"

Terrified, Daphne began to flee. "Help! Help!" she cried. "My father, Peneus, help me!"

Peneus, deus fluminis et pater Daphnes, eam audit et dicit, "Filia mea, tibi auxilium dabo." Et statim Daphne in arborem laurum mutatur.

Peneus, the river god and Daphne's father, heard her and said, "My daughter, I will help you." And immediately Daphne was transformed into a laurel tree.

Apollo, adveniens, tristis est. "O Daphne, cur me fugis?" dicit. Videt arborem laurum et manibus tangit. "Daphne, quamvis in arborem mutata sis, te semper amabo. Hac lauro coronas faciam et semper in capite meo geram."

When Apollo arrived, he was saddened. "O Daphne, why do you flee from me?" he said. He saw the laurel tree and touched it with his hands. "Daphne, though you have been changed into a tree, I will always love you. I will make crowns from this laurel and always wear them on my head."

Ab illo die, Apollo laurum sacram fecit et semper coronam lauri in capite gerit. In silva, ubi Daphne mutata est, Apollo saepe venit, dulcem musicam citharae suae sonans, et de medicina et arte sagittaria docens.

From that day on, Apollo made the laurel sacred and always wore a laurel crown on his head. In the forest where Daphne was transformed, Apollo often came, playing sweet music on his lyre, and teaching about medicine and archery.

Etiam Apollo, post hoc eventum, Pythonem, serpentem magnum et terribilem, interficit. Gentes Graeciae, hoc facto laetae, ludos Pythios in honorem Apollinis instituunt, ubi athletae decertant et poetae carmina dicunt.

After this event, Apollo also killed Python, a great and terrible serpent. The people of Greece, joyful at this deed, established the Pythian Games in honor of Apollo, where athletes compete and poets recite verses.

Apollo, quamquam sagittarius valde bonus est, semper tristis est de amore suo non consecuto. Promittit laurum semper honorare et signum amoris et musicae facere.

Although Apollo was a very skilled archer, he was always saddened by his unfulfilled love. He promised to always honor the laurel and make it a symbol of love and music.

Ita finitur historia de Apolline et Daphne, fabula de amore, metamorphosi et honoribus perpetuis. Apollo, etiam si amor non est consecutus, in arte et musica semper vivit, et Daphne, quamvis in laurum mutata, in memoria hominum et in corona Apollinis semper floret.

Thus ends the story of Apollo and Daphne, a tale of love, transformation, and eternal honors. Though Apollo did not attain love, he lives on in art and music, and Daphne, though changed into a laurel tree, flourishes forever in human memory and in Apollo's crown.

De Phaetonte et Solis Currus

In antiquis temporibus, puer nomine Phaethon erat.

In ancient times, there was a boy named Phaethon.

"Ego sum Solis filius," saepe dicebat. Amici eius non credebant. "Ostende nobis," inquit unus amicus.

"I am the son of the Sun," he often said. His friends did not believe him. "Show us," said one friend.

Phaethon, patrem suum Solem invocare volens, ad palatium Solis ivit. "Pater," clamavit, "si tu vere pater meus es, da mihi signum!"

Phaethon, wanting to call upon his father the Sun, went to the Sun's palace. "Father," he shouted, "if you are truly my father, give me a sign!"

Sol, deus solis, Phaethonta vidit et dixit, "Ego sum pater tuus, Phaethon. Quid vis a me?"

The Sun, god of the sun, saw Phaethon and said, "I am your father, Phaethon. What do you want from me?"

Phaethon, audax, respondit, "Pater, currum tuum regere volo."

Phaethon, boldly, responded, "Father, I want to drive your chariot."

Sol, sollicitus, dixit, "Fili mi, hoc periculosum est. Currus meus non facilis ad regendum est."

The Sun, worried, said, "My son, this is dangerous. My chariot is not easy to drive."

Phaethon tamen insistebat. "Pater, hoc facere possum. Tibi ostendam."

But Phaethon insisted. "Father, I can do this. I will show you."

Sol, amore filii motus, tandem permisit. "Bene," inquit, "sed cave! Currum bene regere debes."

The Sun, moved by love for his son, finally allowed it. "Very well," he said, "but be careful! You must drive the chariot well."

Phaethon, laetus, currum Solis ascendit. Sed mox intellexit se errorem fecisse. Currus, magnis equis tractus, ferebat eum huc illucque. Phaethon territus erat.

Phaethon, happy, ascended the chariot of the Sun. But soon he realized he had made a mistake. The chariot, pulled by mighty horses, was carrying him here and there. Phaethon was terrified.

Curru non bene regendo, terrae ignem adferebat. Montes ardebant, flumina siccabantur.

By not driving the chariot well, he brought fire to the earth. Mountains were burning, and rivers dried up.

Iuppiter, rex deorum, vidit hanc confusionem et iratus erat. "Hoc finire debeo," dixit. Iuppiter Phaethonta fulmine interfecit, mundum salvans.

Jupiter, king of the gods, saw this chaos and was angry. "I must end this," he said. Jupiter killed Phaethon with a lightning bolt, saving the world.

Phaethontis sorores, Heliades appellatae, ubi fratrem mortuum viderunt, valde plorabant. Tantum plorabant, ut in arbores populos mutatae sunt.

Phaethon's sisters, called the Heliades, when they saw their dead brother, wept greatly. They wept so much that they were turned into poplar trees.

Amnis Eridanus, ubi Phaethontis corpus cecidit, eum leniter accepit. Fluminis undae corpus iuvenis tenebant.

The river Eridanus, where Phaethon's body fell, gently received him. The waters of the river held the young man's body.

Sol, pro filio suo luctum habens, diem unum sine sole fecit. "Hodie," dixit Sol, "memoriam filii mei tenebo."

The Sun, mourning for his son, made one day without sunlight. "Today," the Sun said, "I will keep the memory of my son."

Phaethon, in inferis, de audacia sua paenitebat. "O si auscultassem patri meo!" dicebat.

Phaethon, in the underworld, regretted his boldness. "Oh, if only I had listened to my father!" he said.

Terra, post calamitatem, restituitur. Flumina iterum fluebant, arbores rursus virebant.

The earth, after the disaster, was restored. Rivers flowed again, and trees grew green once more.

Memoria Phaethontis manet in arboribus populis. Populi, cum vento moventur, quasi fratrem suum, Phaethonta, plangunt.

The memory of Phaethon remains in the poplar trees. When the poplars move in the wind, it is as if they are mourning their brother, Phaethon.

Ita finitur historia Phaethontis, iuvenis audacis qui currum Solis regere voluit. Haec fabula nos docet de periculis audaciae sine sapientia. Sol, pater amorosus, et Phaethon, filius audax, in memoria hominum et in murmure arborum populi manent.

Thus ends the story of Phaethon, the bold young man who wanted to drive the chariot of the Sun. This tale teaches us about the dangers of boldness without wisdom. The Sun, the loving father, and Phaethon, the daring son, remain in the memory of humans and in the whisper of the poplar trees.

De Io et Iove

In tempore antiquo, Iuppiter, rex deorum, puellam nomine Io amavit.

In ancient times, Jupiter, king of the gods, loved a girl named Io.

Io, pulchra et innocens, in pratis floribus ludebat, nescia deorum in caelo.

Io, beautiful and innocent, was playing in the meadows among the flowers, unaware of the gods in the sky.

Iuppiter, de caelo Io spectans, descendit ad terram. "Salve, Io!" dixit. "Ego sum Iuppiter, rex deorum. Tu valde pulchra es."

Jupiter, watching Io from the sky, descended to the earth. "Greetings, Io!" he said. "I am Jupiter, king of the gods. You are very beautiful."

Io, territa et confusa, respondit, "Cur me, simplicem puellam, laudas, Iuppiter?"

Io, frightened and confused, responded, "Why do you, Jupiter, praise me, a simple girl?"

Iuppiter, amore Io captus, eam protegere volebat. Sed timebat Iunonem, uxorem suam, quae zelotypa erat. Itaque Io in bovem mutavit. "Nunc, Io," dixit Iuppiter, "Iuno te non cognoscet."

Jupiter, captivated by love for Io, wanted to protect her. But he feared Juno, his wife, who was jealous. So, he transformed Io into a cow. "Now, Io," Jupiter said, "Juno will not recognize you."

Iuno, suspiciosa, Iovem de Io interrogavit. "Quis est hic bos, Iuppiter?" rogavit.

Juno, suspicious, questioned Jupiter about Io. "Who is this cow, Jupiter?" she asked.

"Ille bos?" respondit Iuppiter. "Nihil est nisi animal commune."

"That cow?" Jupiter responded. "It is nothing but an ordinary animal."

Iuno, non credens Iovi, Argum, custodem vigilantem, vocavit. "Argus," inquit Iuno, "hoc animal custodi. Noli somnum capere."

Juno, not believing Jupiter, summoned Argus, the watchful guardian. "Argus," Juno said, "guard this animal. Do not fall asleep."

Argus, vir mille oculis, Io custodiebat. Io, tristis et confusa, in forma bovis vivebat.

Argus, a man with a thousand eyes, guarded Io. Io, sad and confused, lived in the form of a cow.

Iuppiter, puellam liberare volens, Mercurium, deum nuntiorum, misit. "Mercuri," inquit Iuppiter, "Argum neca et Io liberare debes."

Jupiter, wishing to free the girl, sent Mercury, the god of messengers. "Mercury," said Jupiter, "you must kill Argus and free Io."

Mercurius, deus callidus, ad Io venit et cithara sua dulcem musicam fecit. Argus, a musica captus, obdormivit. Tum Mercurius eum necavit et Io liberavit.

Mercury, the cunning god, came to Io and played sweet music on his lyre. Argus, captivated by the music, fell asleep. Then Mercury killed him and freed Io.

Io, libera sed adhuc in forma bovis, per multas terras erravit. Per Graeciam, per Italiam, et demum in Aegyptum venit.

Io, free but still in the form of a cow, wandered through many lands. She traveled through Greece, through Italy, and finally came to Egypt.

In Aegypto, Iuppiter eam in formam pristinam restituit. "Io," dixit Iuppiter, "nunc es libera et in forma tua."

In Egypt, Jupiter restored her to her original form. "Io," said Jupiter, "now you are free and in your own form."

Io, laeta, sed etiam sollicita, in Aegypto vixit. Ibi mater Epaphi, filii fortis et magni, facta est.

Io, happy but also worried, lived in Egypt. There she became the mother of Epaphus, a strong and great son.

Gentes Aegypti Io valde amabant. Eam ut deam colebant, et nomen Isis ei dederunt.

The people of Egypt loved Io greatly. They worshiped her as a goddess and gave her the name Isis.

Io et Iuppiter, filium habentes, gaudebant. Epaphus in Aegypto crevit et rex factus est.

Io and Jupiter, having a son, rejoiced. Epaphus grew up in Egypt and became a king.

Io, quae multa passa est, nunc felix erat. Multos homines docebat et sapientia sua omnes adiuvabat.

Io, who had endured many hardships, was now happy. She taught many people and helped everyone with her wisdom.

Iuppiter ex caelo Io spectabat et eam semper amavit. "Io," inquit Iuppiter, "semper in corde meo eris."

Jupiter watched Io from the sky and always loved her. "Io," said Jupiter, "you will always be in my heart."

Ita finitur fabula de Io et Iove, historia plena amoris, transformationis, et fortitudinis. Io, quae multa pericula et mutationes passa est, in Aegypto tanquam dea venerata est. Eius sapientia et experientia multos adiuvabant.

Thus ends the story of Io and Jupiter, a tale full of love, transformation, and strength. Io, who endured many dangers and changes, was worshiped as a goddess in Egypt. Her wisdom and experience helped many.

Epaphus, filius Io et Iovis, in Aegypto rex potens et iustus factus est. Sub eius regno, Aegyptus in pace et prosperitate floruit. Populus Io ut matrem et deam colebat, eius historiam semper meminerunt.

Epaphus, the son of Io and Jupiter, became a powerful and just king in Egypt. Under his reign, Egypt flourished in peace and prosperity. The people worshiped Io as a mother and goddess, and they always remembered her story.

Io, etiam in difficilibus temporibus, fortis et sapientia plena mansit. Multa discens, aliis auxilium dabat. Formam bovis, signum transformationis eius, non timuit, sed ut partem historiae suae amplectebat.

Io, even in difficult times, remained strong and full of wisdom. Learning much, she gave help to others. She did not fear the form of a cow, the symbol of her transformation, but embraced it as part of her story.

Iuppiter, ex alto Olympo, Io et Epaphum semper protegebat. Amor eius ad Io numquam deficiebat, etiam cum erravit.

Jupiter, from high Olympus, always protected Io and Epaphus. His love for Io never failed, even when she wandered.

Historia Io et Iovis nos docet de amore, de mutatione, et de virtute in adversitate. Io, a puella simplici ad deam veneratam evoluta, exemplar est fortitudinis et sapientiae.

The story of Io and Jupiter teaches us about love, transformation, and virtue in adversity. Io, who evolved from a simple girl to a revered goddess, is an example of strength and wisdom.

In Aegypto, Io, nunc Isis appellata, magni honoris erat. Templis eius dedicatis, populus eius beneficia et protectionem orabat.

In Egypt, Io, now called Isis, was greatly honored. With temples dedicated to her, the people prayed for her blessings and protection.

Memoria Io, sicut Isis, in cultura Aegyptia manet, signum feminae fortis quae fata sua superavit et populo suo dux et protectrix facta est. Epaphus, eius filius, rex sapiens et fortis, eiusdem virtutes matris suae ostendit.

The memory of Io, as Isis, remains in Egyptian culture, a symbol of a strong woman who overcame her fate and became a leader and protector for her people. Epaphus, her son, a wise and strong king, displayed the same virtues as his mother.

Sic finit historia Io et Iovis, fabula antiqua, sed semper nova, quae nos docet de transformatione, amore, et fortitudine humana.

Thus ends the story of Io and Jupiter, an ancient tale, but always new, which teaches us about transformation, love, and human strength.

De Acteone et Diana

In tempore antiquo, Actaeon, iuvenis fortis et venator peritus, in silva venabatur.

In ancient times, Actaeon, a strong young man and skilled hunter, was hunting in the forest.

Cum arcu et sagittis, canibusque fidelibus, per silvas et campos errabat. Actaeon silvas amabat et animalia bene sciebat sequi.

With his bow and arrows, and faithful dogs, he wandered through the forests and fields. Actaeon loved the woods and knew well how to track animals.

Die quodam, Actaeon, per silvam ambulans, Dianam, deam venationis et lunae, sine vestimentis in fonte lavantem vidit. Actaeon, stupore captus, stetit et spectavit.

One day, while walking through the forest, Actaeon saw Diana, the goddess of hunting and the moon, bathing naked in a spring. Captivated by amazement, Actaeon stood and watched.

Diana, Actaeonem videntem, irata est. "Cur me spectas, Actaeon?" clamavit. "Nunc poenam dabis!"

Diana, seeing Actaeon, became angry. "Why are you watching me, Actaeon?" she shouted. "Now you will pay the price!"

Subito, Actaeon in cervum mutatus est. Cornua habebat et pedes cervinos. Actaeon, territus, metamorphosin suam non intellegebat. "Quid mihi accidit?" cogitabat.

Suddenly, Actaeon was transformed into a stag. He had antlers and deer's feet. Terrified, Actaeon didn't understand his transformation. "What has happened to me?" he thought.

Actaeon, nunc cervus, fugere conabatur. Sed canes sui, Actaeonem cervum non agnoscentes, eum persecuti sunt. Actaeon timuit et currere temptavit.

Actaeon, now a stag, tried to flee. But his own dogs, not recognizing him as their master, pursued him. Actaeon feared and tried to run.

Canes, Actaeonem sequentes, eum in silva viderunt. Actaeon, cervus factus, ab eis devoratus est. Ipse a propriis canibus captus et laceratus est.

The dogs, following Actaeon, spotted him in the forest. Actaeon, having been turned into a stag, was devoured by them. He was caught and torn apart by his own dogs.

Diana, adhuc irata, silvam reliquit. "Actaeon," inquit, "mea secreta vidisti, poenam dedisti."

Diana, still angry, left the forest. "Actaeon," she said, "you saw my secrets, and you paid the price."

Actaeon, antea venator bonus, nunc in cervum mutatus, vitam suam amisit. Amici eius, Actaeonem quaerentes, eum non invenerunt. "Ubi est Actaeon?" inter se rogabant.

Actaeon, once a great hunter, now turned into a stag, had lost his life. His friends, searching for Actaeon, could not find him. "Where is Actaeon?" they asked one another.

Actaeon, in forma cervi, de vita sua desperabat. Non poterat loqui, non poterat explicare. Silvae, quas semper amavit, nunc locum mortis suae erant.

Actaeon, in the form of a stag, despaired about his life. He could not speak, nor explain what had happened. The forests, which he had always loved, were now the place of his death.

Actaeon, cervus factus, mortem suam non vidit. Canes, feroces et esurientes, eum circumdederunt et devoraverunt. Actaeon, vir fortis et venator peritus, finem tragicum habuit.

Actaeon, transformed into a stag, did not foresee his death. The dogs, fierce and hungry, surrounded him and devoured him. Actaeon, a strong man and skilled hunter, met a tragic end.

Amici Actaeonis, eum diu quaerentes, tandem desistebant. "Forsitan a bestia raptus est," dicebant. Sed veritatem numquam cognoverunt.

Actaeon's friends, searching for him for a long time, eventually gave up. "Perhaps he was taken by a wild beast," they said. But they never knew the truth.

Ita finitur tristis historia Actaeonis, qui, per imprudentiam suam, formam cervi accepit et a canibus suis devoratus est. Diana, dea venationis, severa in suo iudicio fuit, demonstrans gravitatem respectus erga deos.

Thus ends the sad story of Actaeon, who, through his own imprudence, was transformed into a stag and devoured by his own dogs. Diana, goddess of the hunt, was strict in her judgment, showing the importance of respect toward the gods.

Actaeon, in silvis et campis olim felix, exemplum est cautionis in natura et in vita. Eius historia monitionem praebet de periculis arrogantiae et curiositatis in locis sacris.

Actaeon, once happy in the forests and fields, is an example of caution in nature and in life. His story serves as a warning about the dangers of arrogance and curiosity in sacred places.

Silvae, ubi Actaeon venabatur et ubi vitam suam amisit, testimonium sunt de potentia deorum et de mutationibus quas in vita humana inferre possunt. Diana, quamvis dea pulchra, etiam dea potens et terribilis erat, praesertim cum violabantur leges naturae et sacrae.

The forests where Actaeon once hunted and lost his life bear witness to the power of the gods and the transformations they can bring to human lives. Diana, though a beautiful goddess, was also powerful and terrifying, especially when the laws of nature and the sacred were violated.

Amici Actaeonis, post eius mortem, semper eum meminerunt ut venatorem optimum et amicum fidelem. Sed semper mirabantur de eius mysteriosa disparitione.

After Actaeon's death, his friends always remembered him as an excellent hunter and faithful friend. But they always wondered about his mysterious disappearance.

Actaeon, etiam post mortem suam, in memoria venatorum et amantium naturae manet. Exemplar est viri fortis qui, in momento imprudentiae, omnia perdiderat.

Actaeon, even after his death, remains in the memory of hunters and nature lovers. He is an example of a strong man who, in a moment of imprudence, lost everything.

Diana, per hanc historiam, docet homines de respectu et modestia in natura et in sanctis locis. Eius potestas et severitas in fabula Actaeonis clarissime apparent.

Through this story, Diana teaches humans about respect and humility in nature and in sacred places. Her power and severity are most clearly evident in the tale of Actaeon.

Silvae, ubi Actaeon venabatur, nunc loca sunt meditationis et recordationis. Venatores et viatores, per eas ambulantes, saepe cogitant de Actaeone et de vita eius, moniti de periculis quae latent in natura et in ira deorum.

The forests where Actaeon once hunted are now places of meditation and remembrance. Hunters and travelers, walking through them, often think of Actaeon and his life, warned of the dangers that lie in nature and in the wrath of the gods.

Sic finit historia Actaeonis, tristis sed plena doctrina. Narratio eius, per saecula, monitum est de reverentia quae debetur naturae et divinis, et de fine tragico qui sequi potest cum haec oblita sunt.

Thus ends the story of Actaeon, sad but full of lessons. His tale, throughout the ages, is a reminder of the reverence owed to nature and the divine, and of the tragic end that can follow when these are forgotten.

De Europa et Iove

In tempore antiquo, Iuppiter, rex deorum, in caelo sedebat et terram spectabat.

In ancient times, Jupiter, king of the gods, sat in the sky and watched the earth.

Subito, puellam pulchram vidit. "Europa!" exclamavit. "Illa puella pulchra est!"

Suddenly, he saw a beautiful girl. "Europa!" he exclaimed. "That girl is beautiful!"

Europa, filia regis Phoeniciae, in litore ambulabat, flores colligens. Nesciebat deum Iovem eam spectare.

Europa, the daughter of the king of Phoenicia, was walking on the shore, gathering flowers. She did not know that Jupiter was watching her.

Iuppiter, amore Europae captus, ad terram descendit. Sed formam tauri elegit, ne eum Europa timeret. "Ego tauro me mutabo," cogitavit.

Jupiter, captivated by love for Europa, descended to the earth. But he chose the form of a bull so that Europa would not fear him. "I will change into a bull," he thought.

Europa, tauro albo in litore videndo, non timuit. Tauro pulchro et mansueto confidebat. "Quam pulcher es!" inquit Europa, tauro adpropinquans.

When Europa saw the white bull on the shore, she was not afraid. She trusted the beautiful and gentle bull. "How beautiful you are!" Europa said, approaching the bull.

Iuppiter, in forma tauri, Europam suaviter adspexit. Europa, tauro confidens, in dorso eius ascendit.

Jupiter, in the form of a bull, gazed softly at Europa. Trusting the bull, Europa climbed onto its back.

Subito, Iuppiter, adhuc in forma tauri, cum Europa ad Cretam navigavit. Europa, in dorso tauri sedens, mirabatur. "Quo me ducis?" rogavit.

Suddenly, Jupiter, still in the form of a bull, sailed with Europa to Crete. Sitting on the bull's back, Europa was amazed. "Where are you taking me?" she asked.

Iuppiter, in Creta, formam suam veram revelavit. "Ego sum Iuppiter, rex deorum," dixit. "Te amo et tecum in Creta manere volo."

In Crete, Jupiter revealed his true form. "I am Jupiter, king of the gods," he said. "I love you and want you to stay with me in Crete."

Europa, Iovis identitatem discens, mirabatur. "Tu es Iuppiter?" inquit. "Cur me elegisti?"

Learning Jupiter's identity, Europa was amazed. "You are Jupiter?" she asked. "Why did you choose me?"

Iuppiter, "Quia te amo," respondit. "Et tibi protectionem semper promitto."

Jupiter replied, "Because I love you. And I promise you protection forever."

Europa, in Creta, tres filios Iovis peperit: Minos, Rhadamanthus, et Sarpedon. Minos postea rex Cretae factus est, vir sapiens et potens.

In Crete, Europa bore three sons to Jupiter: Minos, Rhadamanthus, and Sarpedon. Minos later became the king of Crete, a wise and powerful man.

Europa, nomen suum continenti dedit. Terra, ubi nata est, "Europa" appellata est in honorem eius.

Europa gave her name to a continent. The land where she was born was called "Europe" in her honor.

Iuppiter, Europam honorans, eam reginam novae terrae fecit. Europa, a tauri dorso non cadens, fortis et audax erat.

Honoring Europa, Jupiter made her the queen of a new land. Europa, who did not fall from the bull's back, was strong and bold.

Europa, in Creta, novam vitam coepit. "Hic regina ero," cogitavit. Et terra eius pulchra et fertilis erat.

Europa began a new life in Crete. "Here I will be queen," she thought. And her land was beautiful and fertile.

Minos, Europae filius, Minotaurum, monstrum terribile, habuit. Europa, nepotem suum mirabatur. "Quam mira sunt fata!" inquit.

Minos, Europa's son, had the Minotaur, a terrible monster. Europa marveled at her grandson. "How strange are the fates!" she said.

Europa, de adventu suo in Cretam semper mirabatur. "Vita mea mirabilis est," cogitabat. "A puella Phoenicia ad reginam Cretae!"

Europa always marveled at her arrival in Crete. "My life is wonderful," she thought. "From a Phoenician girl to the queen of Crete!"

Europa, ab Iove semper amata et honorata, in historia manet. Exemplar est feminae fortis, quae nova vita et nova terra incipit.

Europa, always loved and honored by Jupiter, remains in history. She is an example of a strong woman who starts a new life and a new land.

Sic finitur fabula Europae et Iovis, historia de amore, transformatione, et regno. Europa, regina fortis et audax, in memoria hominum manet, signum feminae quae fata sua superavit et regina nova terrae facta est.

Thus ends the story of Europa and Jupiter, a tale of love, transformation, and kingdom. Europa, a strong and bold queen, remains in human memory, a symbol of a woman who overcame her fate and became queen of a new land.

Iuppiter, in forma tauri, Europam ad novam vitam et ad novam terram duxit. Eius amor et protectio Europae viam novam aperuerunt.

Jupiter, in the form of a bull, led Europa to a new life and a new land. His love and protection opened a new path for Europa.

In Creta, Europa reginam sapientem et benignam se praebuit. Sub eius regimine, Creta floruit et prosperitatem magnam habuit.

In Crete, Europa proved to be a wise and kind queen. Under her rule, Crete flourished and had great prosperity.

Europa, in insula Creta, culturae et artibus studebat. Eius regnum exemplar erat sapientiae et pacis. Populus eam amabat et honorabat ut matrem et reginam.

Europa, on the island of Crete, studied culture and the arts. Her kingdom was an example of wisdom and peace. The people loved and honored her as mother and queen.

Minos, Europae filius, leges iustas et sapientes in Creta constituit. Eius regnum longum et prosperum erat, et in historia Cretae magni momenti est.

Minos, Europa's son, established just and wise laws in Crete. His reign was long and prosperous, and he is of great importance in the history of Crete.

Rhadamanthus et Sarpedon, alii filii Europae et Iovis, etiam in historia Cretae et Graeciae noti sunt. Utrique in suis regionibus iustitiam et sapientiam promovebant.

Rhadamanthus and Sarpedon, the other sons of Europa and Jupiter, are also known in the history of Crete and Greece. Both promoted justice and wisdom in their regions.

Europa, cum filiis suis, culturae Cretae magnam influentiam habuit. Artes, leges, et scientiae sub eis floruerunt, et Creta facta est unum ex maxime civilizatis locis in mundo antiquo.

Europa, along with her sons, had great influence on the culture of Crete. Arts, laws, and sciences flourished under them, and Crete became one of the most civilized places in the ancient world.

Minotaurus, in labyrintho a Daedalo factus, monstrum et mysterium Cretae erat. Europa, quamvis Minotauri avia esset, cum Theseo consilium fecit ut monstrum vinceretur.

The Minotaur, built by Daedalus in the labyrinth, was a monster and mystery of Crete. Although Europa was the Minotaur's grandmother, she advised Theseus to defeat the monster.

Europa, per vitam suam, multa mirabilia vidit et multas res novas didicit. Semper aperta erat ad discendum et ad explorandum.

Throughout her life, Europa saw many wonders and learned many new things. She was always open to learning and exploring.

Iuppiter, eam semper amans, a caelo Europam custodiebat. Eius amor et protectio signum erant dei potentis et amorosi.

Jupiter, always loving her, watched over Europa from the sky. His love and protection were signs of a powerful and loving god.

Europa, in fine vitae suae, retrospectum fecit et de incredibili itinere suo cogitavit. "A puella ad reginam, a Phoenicia ad Cretam, a mortalibus ad deos," inquit. "Vita mea plena est miraculis et amoris."

At the end of her life, Europa looked back and thought about her incredible journey. "From girl to queen, from Phoenicia to Crete, from mortals to gods," she said. "My life is full of miracles and love."

Sic finit historia de Europa et Iove, fabula antiqua de amore, metamorphosi, et regno. Europa, in historia et in mythologia, semper manet ut exemplar audaciae, sapientiae, et fortitudinis.

Thus ends the story of Europa and Jupiter, an ancient tale of love, transformation, and kingdom. Europa, in history and mythology, remains forever as an example of boldness, wisdom, and strength.

De Cadmo et Dracone

Cadmus, filius regis Phoeniciae, sororem suam Europam quaerebat.

Cadmus, the son of the king of Phoenicia, was searching for his sister Europa.

Europa a Iove rapta fuerat, et Cadmus eam per multas terras et maria sequi voluit.

Europa had been abducted by Jupiter, and Cadmus wanted to follow her through many lands and seas.

Cadmus, incertus quo iret, oraculum Delphicum consuluit. "Oraculum," rogavit Cadmus, "ubi sororem meam inveniam?"

Cadmus, unsure of where to go, consulted the Delphic oracle. "Oracle," asked Cadmus, "where will I find my sister?"

Oraculum respondit, "Non Europam quaerere debes, sed urbem novam condere." Cadmus, oraculi verba audiens, iter suum mutavit.

The oracle replied, "You must not search for Europa, but rather found a new city." Hearing the oracle's words, Cadmus changed his path.

Cadmus in Boeotiam venit, ubi urbem condere iubebatur. Sed in loco, ubi urbem condere voluit, draconem ingentem et terribilem invenit.

Cadmus arrived in Boeotia, where he was commanded to found a city. But in the place where he wanted to build the city, he found a huge and terrible dragon.

Draco, qui fontem sacrum custodiebat, Cadmum impetum fecit. Cadmus, audax et fortis, draconem gladio suo interfecit.

The dragon, which was guarding the sacred spring, attacked Cadmus. Cadmus, brave and strong, killed the dragon with his sword.

Postea, Cadmus, oraculi monitu, dentes draconis in terra serit. Mirabile dictu, ex dentibus homines armati nascuntur. Hi homines Sparti appellati sunt.

Afterwards, Cadmus, following the oracle's advice, sowed the dragon's teeth in the ground. Amazingly, from the teeth, armed men were born. These men were called the Sparti.

Cum auxilio Spartorum, Cadmus urbem Thebas condidit. Thebae, urbs nova et fortis, celeriter crevit et floruit.

With the help of the Sparti, Cadmus founded the city of Thebes. Thebes, a new and strong city, quickly grew and flourished.

Cadmus Harmoniam, filiam Martis et Veneris, in matrimonium duxit. Nuptiae eorum magnificae et laetae erant. Omnes dei ad nuptias venerunt et dona dederunt.

Cadmus married Harmonia, the daughter of Mars and Venus. Their wedding was magnificent and joyful. All the gods attended the wedding and gave gifts.

Cadmus et Harmonia filios habuerunt, qui in Thebis reges et heroes futuri erant. Eorum familia et posteri magni in historia Graeca fuerunt.

Cadmus and Harmonia had children who would become kings and heroes in Thebes. Their family and descendants were important in Greek history.

Post multos annos, Cadmus et Harmonia in serpentes mutati sunt. Non tristes aut timidi, sed parati ad novam vitam. Eorum mutatio mirabilis fuit.

After many years, Cadmus and Harmonia were transformed into serpents. They were not sad or fearful, but ready for a new life. Their transformation was miraculous.

Cadmus, in Thebis regnans, urbi magnam famam et prosperitatem attulit. Sua sapientia et virtute, Thebae una ex maximis urbibus Graeciae factae sunt.

Cadmus, ruling in Thebes, brought great fame and prosperity to the city. Through his wisdom and virtue, Thebes became one of the greatest cities in Greece.

Cadmus, sator stirpis regiae Thebanorum, magni honoris in historia erat. Eius posteri multos annos in Thebis regnaverunt.

Cadmus, the founder of the royal Theban lineage, was of great honor in history. His descendants ruled in Thebes for many years.

Cadmus, tamen, semper luctum pro fratre suo, qui a dracone occisus erat, habuit. Fratris memoria in corde suo semper erat.

However, Cadmus always mourned for his brother, who had been killed by the dragon. The memory of his brother was always in his heart.

In fine vitae suae, Cadmus et Harmonia in deos assumpti sunt. Eorum vita, plena laborum et triumphorum, exemplar erat fortitudinis et constantiae.

At the end of their lives, Cadmus and Harmonia were taken up as gods. Their life, full of struggles and triumphs, was an example of strength and perseverance.

Thus ends the story of Cadmus and the Dragon, a tale of virtue, transformation, and the founding of a city. Cadmus, a strong and wise man, and Harmonia, his wife, remain in the memory of humans and in Greek history. Their life and deeds are examples of courage, love, and the founding of a great city.

De Nilo

In antiqua terra Aegypti, magnus et mirabilis fluvius est, cui nomen Nilus.

In the ancient land of Egypt, there is a great and marvelous river called the Nile.

Nilus per longam terram Aegypti fluit et vitam fert. Nilus est non solum fluvius, sed etiam fons vitae et benedictionis.

The Nile flows through the long land of Egypt and brings life. The Nile is not just a river, but also a source of life and blessing.

Agricolae ad Nilum laborant. Terra iuxta Nilum fertilis est, quia Nilus aquam et nutrimentum dat. "Gratias tibi, Nilo," dicunt agricolae, "quia frumentum et alia alimenta nobis fers." Nilus agricolis frumentum, legumina, et multa alia alimenta dat.

Farmers work near the Nile. The land next to the Nile is fertile because the Nile provides water and nutrients. "Thank you, Nile," the farmers say, "for bringing us grain and other food." The Nile gives farmers grain, vegetables, and many other foods.

In Aegypto, multae urbes et villae ad Nilum sunt. Homines prope Nilum habitant quia aqua vitae necessaria est. "Nilus nobis vitam dat," dicit mulier in villa. "Sine Nilo, vivere non possumus."

In Egypt, there are many cities and villages near the Nile. People live near the Nile because water is necessary for life. "The Nile gives us life," says a woman in the village. "Without the Nile, we cannot live."

Nilus non solum aquam bibendam fert, sed etiam terram irrigat. In aestate, Nilus crescit et decrescit, secundum tempora anni. "Nilus nunc crescit," dicit puer, "et agri nostri irrigabuntur."

The Nile not only provides drinking water but also irrigates the land. In the summer, the Nile rises and falls according to the seasons. "The Nile is rising now," says a boy, "and our fields will be watered."

Nilus etiam est domus multorum animalium aquatilium. Pisces in Nilo natant, et aves aquae prope Nilum volitant. "Vide pisces in Nilo!" exclamat puer. "Nilus plenus est vita."

The Nile is also home to many aquatic animals. Fish swim in the Nile, and water birds fly near the Nile. "Look at the fish in the Nile!" exclaims the boy. "The Nile is full of life."

Aegyptii Nilum colunt et celebrant. Festi et ritus ad Nili honorem fiunt. "Nilus est magnus et sanctus," dicit sacerdos. "Eum honoramus et celebramus."

The Egyptians worship and celebrate the Nile. Festivals and rituals are held in honor of the Nile. "The Nile is great and sacred," says a priest. "We honor and celebrate it."

Nilus in historia Aegypti magni momenti est. Aegyptii sciebant se sine Nilo non vivere posse. "Nilus est cor Aegypti," inquit senex. "Historia nostra cum Nilo incipit."

The Nile is of great importance in the history of Egypt. The Egyptians knew they could not live without the Nile. "The Nile is the heart of Egypt," says an old man. "Our history begins with the Nile."

Nilus est etiam symbolum vitae et fecunditatis. "Nilus," dicit poeta, "est fons vitae, fons omnium bonorum in Aegypto." Nilus est fluvius qui vitam dat, qui terram fecundat, qui Aegyptum vivam et florentem facit.

The Nile is also a symbol of life and fertility. "The Nile," says a poet, "is the source of life, the source of all good things in Egypt." The Nile is the river that gives life, fertilizes the land, and makes Egypt vibrant and flourishing.

In cultura Aegyptia, Nilus magnopere celebratur. Nilus in picturis, carminibus, et fabulis apparet. "Nilus in arte nostra vivit," dicit artifex. "Eum in picturis et sculpturis nostris celebramus."

In Egyptian culture, the Nile is greatly celebrated. The Nile appears in paintings, poems, and stories. "The Nile lives in our art," says an artist. "We celebrate it in our paintings and sculptures."

Homines ex Nilo aquam hauriunt, cum ea coquunt et lavant. "Nilus nobis aquam puram dat," dicit materfamilias. "Sine ea, vita difficilior esset."

People draw water from the Nile, using it for cooking and washing. "The Nile gives us clean water," says a mother. "Without it, life would be harder."

Aegyptii, Nilum colentes, semper grati sunt pro eius donis. Festi et celebrationes ad Nili honorem saepe fiunt. "In festis Nili, gratias agimus et laetamur," inquit adolescens. "Nilus est pars vitae nostrae."

The Egyptians, who revere the Nile, are always grateful for its gifts. Festivals and celebrations are often held in honor of the Nile. "During the Nile festivals, we give thanks and rejoice," says a young man. "The Nile is a part of our life."

Nilus, cum fluctibus suis, terram fertilitate implet. Fluctus Nili, quos Aegyptii "inundationem" vocant, terram ad culturas parant.

"Inundatio Nili agros nostros parat," dicit agricola. "Sine ea, terra nostra arida esset."

The Nile, with its waves, fills the land with fertility. The floods of the Nile, which the Egyptians call "inundation," prepare the land for crops. "The flood of the Nile prepares our fields," says a farmer. "Without it, our land would be dry."

In historia Aegypti, Nilus est fons prosperitatis et culturae. Aegyptii ad Nilum multas urbes magnificas aedificaverunt. "Urbes nostrae iuxta Nilum florent," inquit magistratus. "Nilus est fons prosperitatis nostrae."

In the history of Egypt, the Nile is the source of prosperity and culture. The Egyptians built many magnificent cities along the Nile. "Our cities thrive by the Nile," says an official. "The Nile is the source of our prosperity."

Nilus etiam est via communicationis et commercii. Naviculae in Nilo navigant, merces et homines ferentes. "Per Nilum, ad diversas terrae partes navigamus," inquit nauta. "Nilus est via nostra."

The Nile is also a route of communication and commerce. Boats sail on the Nile, carrying goods and people. "Through the Nile, we sail to different parts of the land," says a sailor. "The Nile is our way."

In fine, Nilus non solum fluvius est, sed etiam symbolus et cor Aegypti. Aegyptii Nilum amant et reverentur. "Nilus est donum dei," dicit Aegyptius. "Eum amamus et in corde nostro tenemus."

In the end, the Nile is not just a river, but also a symbol and the heart of Egypt. The Egyptians love and revere the Nile. "The Nile is a gift from the gods," says an Egyptian. "We love it and hold it in our hearts."

Sic finitur descriptio Nili, fluvii magni et benedicti, qui per terram Aegypti fluit et vitam et prosperitatem fert. Nilus in corde Aegyptiorum et in historia humanitatis semper manebit, fluvius magnus et sanctus, fons vitae et benedictionis.

Thus ends the description of the Nile, the great and blessed river, which flows through the land of Egypt and brings life and prosperity. The Nile will always remain in the hearts of the Egyptians and in human history, a great and sacred river, a source of life and blessing.

De Nymphae et Satyris

In antiquis silvis et pulchris fluminibus, nymphae, spiritus naturae, habitant.

In ancient forests and beautiful rivers, nymphs, spirits of nature, dwell.

Formosae et immortales, per silvas ludentes et in ripis aquarum saltantes, nymphae vitam in natura celebrant.

Beautiful and immortal, playing through the forests and dancing on the riverbanks, the nymphs celebrate life in nature.

"Nymphae sunt custodes fluminum et silvarum," dicit vetus silvae. "Eae naturam et animalia protegunt." Nymphae curam gerunt pro omnibus viventibus in silvis et aquis.

"The nymphs are the guardians of the rivers and forests," says an elder of the woods. "They protect nature and animals." Nymphs take care of all living things in the forests and waters.

Satyri, semihomines et semibestiae, etiam in silvis habitant. Gaudia vitae amantes, satyri saepe cum nymphis ludunt et eas amant. "Satyri semper nymphas sequuntur," ridet satyrus. "Amor et iocus vita nostra sunt."

Satyrs, half-human and half-beast, also live in the forests. Lovers of life's joys, satyrs often play with and love the nymphs. "Satyrs always follow nymphs," laughs a satyr. "Love and play are our life."

Sed nymphae saepe a satyris fugiunt, ludentes et ridentes. "Satyri ludicri sunt," ridet nympha. "Sed nos liberae et silvaticae sumus."

But the nymphs often flee from the satyrs, playing and laughing. "Satyrs are playful," laughs a nymph. "But we are free and wild."

Interdum, nymphae et satyri festa in silvis celebrant. Musica, cantus, saltatio, et risus festas noctes implet. "Festae noctes sunt tempora gaudii," exclamat satyrus. "Musica et saltatio cor nostrum laetificant."

Sometimes, the nymphs and satyrs celebrate festivals in the woods. Music, song, dance, and laughter fill the festive nights. "Festive nights are times of joy," exclaims a satyr. "Music and dancing make our hearts happy."

Nymphae, cum potestate super aquas, flumina et lacus curant. "Aquae sunt domus nostra," dicit nympha. "Eas protegimus et amamus."

The nymphs, with power over the waters, care for rivers and lakes. "The waters are our home," says a nymph. "We protect and love them."

Satyri, amici Dionysi, dei vini, festas et lascivas vitas ducunt. "Dionysus dux noster est," inquit satyrus. "Vita nostra est celebratio."

Satyrs, friends of Dionysus, the god of wine, live festive and wild lives. "Dionysus is our leader," says a satyr. "Our life is a celebration."

In fabulis Graecis et Romanis, nymphae et satyri saepe apparuerunt. "Fabulae nostrae homines de natura et libertate docent," narrat nympha.

In Greek and Roman stories, nymphs and satyrs often appeared. "Our tales teach humans about nature and freedom," says a nymph.

Nymphae in artibus, ut in picturis et sculpturis, depictae sunt. "Forma et pulchritudo nymphae in arte vivunt," dicit artifex.

Nymphs are depicted in the arts, such as in paintings and sculptures. "The form and beauty of the nymphs live on in art," says an artist.

Satyri sunt symbola naturae et libertatis. "Satyri spiritus liberi sunt," dicit poeta. "Ei naturae et vitae gaudia repraesentant."

Satyrs are symbols of nature and freedom. "Satyrs are free spirits," says a poet. "They represent the joys of nature and life."

Interdum, nymphae et satyri amicitiam habent, naturam et vitam celebrantes. "Amicitia nostra est symbolum harmoniae," dicit nympha.

Sometimes, the nymphs and satyrs share friendship, celebrating nature and life. "Our friendship is a symbol of harmony," says a nymph.

Nymphae et satyri partem magnam in mythologia Graeca et Romana habent. Eorum fabulae de vita, natura, amore, et libertate narrantur.

Nymphs and satyrs play a major role in Greek and Roman mythology. Their stories tell of life, nature, love, and freedom.

"Vita in silvis est plena miris et pulchritudinibus," dicit nympha. "Natura est domus et cor nostrum."

"Life in the woods is full of wonders and beauty," says a nymph. "Nature is our home and heart."

Satyri, cum tympanis et tibiis, per silvas saltant et cantant. "Musica est lingua nostra," inquit satyrus. "Per eam, vitam et naturam laudamus."

Satyrs, with drums and pipes, dance and sing through the forests. "Music is our language," says a satyr. "Through it, we praise life and nature."

Nymphae, fluminibus et fontibus praesidentes, aquarum sonos et melodias audiunt. "Aqua est musica nostra," dicit nympha. "Ea nobis pacem et inspirationem dat."

The nymphs, presiding over rivers and fountains, listen to the sounds and melodies of the waters. "Water is our music," says a nymph. "It gives us peace and inspiration."

In noctibus lunatis, nymphae et satyri sub lumine lunae festa magna celebrant. "Luna nostra dea est," exclamat nympha. "Ea nos ad festa vocat."

On moonlit nights, nymphs and satyrs celebrate great festivals under the light of the moon. "The moon is our goddess," exclaims a nymph. "She calls us to the festivities."

Satyri, silvas et montes peragrant, semper in motu et gaudio. "Satyri naturae filii sunt," narrat viator. "Eorum vita est perpetuum festum."

Satyrs wander through forests and mountains, always in motion and joy. "Satyrs are children of nature," says a traveler. "Their life is a perpetual festival."

Nymphae, naturae pulchritudinem et mysteria custodientes, hominibus naturae mirabilia ostendunt. "Nymphae sunt magistrae naturae," dicit philosophus. "Ab eis, naturae secreta discimus."

Nymphs, guarding the beauty and mysteries of nature, reveal nature's wonders to humans. "Nymphs are the teachers of nature," says a philosopher. "From them, we learn the secrets of nature."

Satyri, Dionyso in festis comitantes, vinum et laetitiam ad homines portant. "Vinum est donum Dionysi," inquit satyrus. "Eo, vitam celebramus."

Satyrs, accompanying Dionysus in festivals, bring wine and joy to humans. "Wine is Dionysus' gift," says a satyr. "With it, we celebrate life."

Nymphae et satyri, in harmonia cum natura, exemplum vitae naturalis et liberae praebent. "Nymphae et satyri nos docent vivere in pace cum natura," dicit poeta. "Eorum fabulae sunt lectiones vitae."

Nymphs and satyrs, in harmony with nature, provide an example of a natural and free life. "Nymphs and satyrs teach us to live in peace with nature," says a poet. "Their stories are lessons of life."

Sic finitur descriptio nympharum et satyrorum, spirituum naturae qui in silvis et fluminibus habitant. Eorum vita est celebratio naturae, libertatis, et gaudii. In mythologia et cultura, nymphae et satyri exemplum vivendi in harmonia cum mundo naturali praebent.

Thus ends the description of the nymphs and satyrs, spirits of nature who live in forests and rivers. Their life is a celebration of nature, freedom, and joy. In mythology and culture, nymphs and satyrs provide an example of living in harmony with the natural world.

De Pan et Syrinx

In antiquis temporibus, in silvis Graeciae, deus silvarum, Pan nomine, vivebat.

In ancient times, in the forests of Greece, a god of the woods named Pan lived.

Pan erat deus naturae et pastorum, semper cum caprinis pedibus et cornibus. Pan musicam amabat et fistulam semper portabat.

Pan was the god of nature and shepherds, always with goat-like feet and horns. Pan loved music and always carried his flute.

Unum diem, Pan Syrinx, pulchram nympham, vidit et statim eam amavit. Syrinx, formosa et libera, per silvas et flumina vagabatur.

One day, Pan saw Syrinx, a beautiful nymph, and immediately loved her. Syrinx, beautiful and free, wandered through the forests and rivers.

Pan, amore captus, Syrinx sequi coepit. Sed Syrinx, deum silvarum videns, timuit et fugere coepit. "Cur me sequeris, Pan?" clamavit Syrinx. "Ego libera sum et sola esse volo."

Pan, captivated by love, began to follow Syrinx. But Syrinx, seeing the god of the woods, became afraid and started to flee. "Why are you following me, Pan?" cried Syrinx. "I am free and I want to be alone."

Pan, tamen, non desistebat et Syrinx per silvas secutus est. Syrinx, fugiens, ad flumen venit et auxilium deorum petivit. "O dei, adiuvate me!" exclamavit. "Nolo a Pano capi!"

Pan, however, did not give up and pursued Syrinx through the woods. Fleeing, Syrinx came to a river and called upon the gods for help. "Oh gods, help me!" she exclaimed. "I don't want to be caught by Pan!"

Subito, mirum factum est. Syrinx in arundinem mutata est. Pan, ad flumen perveniens, Syrinx quaesivit sed solum arundines invenit.

Suddenly, something miraculous happened. Syrinx was transformed into a reed. When Pan arrived at the river, he searched for Syrinx but found only reeds.

Pan, tristis Syrinx non inveniens, arundinem cepit et fistulam fecit. "Etsi te non habeo, Syrinx," dixit Pan, "tamen in hac fistula canam."

Pan, sad that he could not find Syrinx, took a reed and made a flute. "Even though I do not have you, Syrinx," said Pan, "I will still play your music on this flute."

Pan, fistulam suam sonans, dulcem musicam per silvas spargebat. Musica Panis, suavis et melodiosa, per omnes silvas audita est.

Pan, playing his flute, spread sweet music through the forests. Pan's music, soft and melodious, was heard throughout the woods.

Pan et Syrinx in fabulis Graecis et Romanis saepe narrati sunt. Eorum historia est fabula amoris, musicae, et libertatis.

Pan and Syrinx are often told about in Greek and Roman myths. Their story is a tale of love, music, and freedom.

Pan, deus naturae, cum fistula sua, magiam naturae exprimebat. Pastores et venatores, musicam eius audientes, in silvis laeti erant.

Pan, the god of nature, with his flute, expressed the magic of nature. Shepherds and hunters, hearing his music, were happy in the woods.

Syrinx, nunc arundo, a pastoribus et venatoribus colitur. Eius mutatio in arundinem symbolum libertatis et mutationis est.

Syrinx, now a reed, is honored by shepherds and hunters. Her transformation into a reed is a symbol of freedom and change.

Historia Panis et Syrinx origines musicae rusticae explicat. Musica Panis naturae sonos et harmoniam exprimebat.

The story of Pan and Syrinx explains the origins of rustic music. Pan's music expressed the sounds and harmony of nature.

In arte Graeca et Romana, Pan et Syrinx magni momenti sunt. Eorum imagines in picturis, sculpturis, et carminibus apparuerunt.

In Greek and Roman art, Pan and Syrinx are of great importance. Their images appeared in paintings, sculptures, and poems.

"Pan et Syrinx," dicit artifex, "in arte nostra vivunt. Eorum fabula inspiratio est." Pan, fistulam suam sonans, et Syrinx, pulchra nympha mutata, in arte et cultura perennem locum habent.

"Pan and Syrinx," says an artist, "live on in our art. Their story is an inspiration." Pan, playing his flute, and Syrinx, the beautiful nymph transformed, hold a permanent place in art and culture.

Sic finitur historia de Pan et Syrinx, fabula antiqua de amore, musica, et libertate. Pan, deus silvarum et musicae, et Syrinx, nympha libertatis, in memoria hominum et in naturae cantu semper manebunt.

Thus ends the story of Pan and Syrinx, an ancient tale of love, music, and freedom. Pan, the god of the woods and music, and Syrinx, the nymph of freedom, will forever remain in the memory of humans and in the song of nature.

Eorum fabula, inter arbores susurrans et in aquis murmurans, nos docet de amoris potentia, de naturae pulchritudine, et de libertatis valore.

Their story, whispering among the trees and murmuring in the waters, teaches us about the power of love, the beauty of nature, and the value of freedom.

Pan, cum fistula sua, silvas et campos animavit. "Musica mea," inquit Pan, "est donum naturae et expressio animae meae." Per fistulam, Pan cum natura loquebatur, et silvae et montes eius cantibus resonabant.

Pan, with his flute, brought life to the forests and fields. "My music," said Pan, "is a gift of nature and an expression of my soul." Through his flute, Pan spoke with nature, and the woods and mountains echoed his songs.

Syrinx, etsi in arundinem mutata, spiritum suum libertatem retinebat. Flumina et venti eius historiam narrabant. "Etsi forma mea mutata est," susurrat Syrinx, "spiritus meus liber manet."

Syrinx, although transformed into a reed, retained her spirit of freedom. The rivers and winds told her story. "Even though my form has changed," whispers Syrinx, "my spirit remains free."

Pastores et venatores, Panem et Syrinx venerantes, ad eorum loca sacra veniebant. "Pan nos protegit," dicit pastor. "Syrinx nos inspirat," inquit venator. Eorum memoria in corde rusticorum vivit.

Shepherds and hunters, venerating Pan and Syrinx, would come to their sacred places. "Pan protects us," says a shepherd. "Syrinx inspires us," says a hunter. Their memory lives in the hearts of the rural people.

Pan, per silvas errans, semper Syrinx memorabat. Fistula eius, dulces melodias creans, erat monumentum amoris aeterni. "In fistula mea," dicit Pan, "Syrinx aeternum vivit."

Pan, wandering through the woods, always remembered Syrinx. His flute, creating sweet melodies, was a monument to eternal love. "In my flute," says Pan, "Syrinx lives forever."

Artes, fabulae, et carmina, Panis et Syrinx historiam per saecula portaverunt. "Eorum fabula," narrat poeta, "est carmen naturae et amoris, quod numquam moritur."

The arts, stories, and poems have carried the history of Pan and Syrinx through the centuries. "Their story," says a poet, "is a song of nature and love that never dies."

De Iove et Lycaone

In antiqua Graecia, Iuppiter, rex deorum, terram visitavit ut hominum mores perspiceret.

In ancient Greece, Jupiter, king of the gods, visited the earth to observe the behavior of humans.

In Arcadia, regno Lycaonis, Iuppiter venit, humana forma indutus.

In Arcadia, the kingdom of Lycaon, Jupiter arrived, disguised in human form.

Lycaon, rex Arcadiae, notus erat pro crudelitate sua. "Lycaon est rex crudelis et impius," dicebant homines. "Eum timemus."

Lycaon, king of Arcadia, was known for his cruelty. "Lycaon is a cruel and impious king," the people said. "We fear him."

Cum Iuppiter, ut hospes, ad Lycaonem venit, Lycaon eum decipere conatus est. "Videamus an hic vere deus sit," cogitavit Lycaon. "Si mortalem naturam habet, eum decipiam."

When Jupiter came to Lycaon as a guest, Lycaon tried to deceive him. "Let's see if this one is truly a god," thought Lycaon. "If he has mortal nature, I will deceive him."

Lycaon, vescendi causa, hominem occidit et Iovi cibum humanum praebuit. Iuppiter, fraude cognita, iratus factus est. "Lycaon," inquit Iuppiter, "pro tua impietate poenas dabis!"

Lycaon, for the purpose of dining, killed a man and offered human flesh to Jupiter. Jupiter, recognizing the deceit, became enraged. "Lycaon," said Jupiter, "you will pay for your impiety!"

Subito, Lycaon in lupum mutatus est. "Nunc," dixit Iuppiter, "forma tua crudelitatem tuam exprimit." Lycaon, lupus factus, in silvas fugit.

Suddenly, Lycaon was transformed into a wolf. "Now," said Jupiter, "your form expresses your cruelty." Lycaon, now a wolf, fled into the woods.

Lycaonis metamorphosis exemplar est superbiae et crudelitatis. "Lycaon in lupum mutatus est quia crudelis erat," narrabant homines. "Iustitia deorum est severa."

Lycaon's transformation is an example of pride and cruelty. "Lycaon was turned into a wolf because he was cruel," the people said. "The justice of the gods is severe."

Iuppiter, hominum impietate commotus, ad caelum rediit et deorum concilium vocavit. "Hominum mores intolerabiles sunt," dixit Iuppiter. "Consilium capere debemus."

Jupiter, disturbed by the impiety of humans, returned to the heavens and called a council of the gods. "The behavior of humans is intolerable," said Jupiter. "We must make a decision."

Dei, Iovis verbis auditis, de diluvio decernunt. "Diluvium mundum purgabit," dixerunt dei. "Nova initia fient."

The gods, hearing Jupiter's words, decided on a flood. "The flood will cleanse the world," said the gods. "New beginnings will be made."

Diluvium ingens factum est. Aquae omnia operuerunt, terras, montes, urbes. Sed Deucalion et Pyrrha, iusti et pii, superesse potuerunt.

A great flood occurred. Waters covered everything, lands, mountains, and cities. But Deucalion and Pyrrha, just and pious, were able to survive.

Deucalion et Pyrrha, post diluvium, novam humanitatem creaverunt. "Dei nobis secundam chancem dederunt," dixit Deucalion. "Humanitatem meliorem faciemus."

Deucalion and Pyrrha, after the flood, created a new humanity. "The gods have given us a second chance," said Deucalion. "We will make a better humanity."

Lycaonis metamorphosis et diluvium monitum fuerunt hominibus. "Dei nos docent," dixit Pyrrha, "iustitiam et pietatem esse necessarias."

Lycaon's transformation and the flood were a warning to humans. "The gods teach us," said Pyrrha, "that justice and piety are necessary."

Lycaonis historia, in mythologia Graeca et Romana narrata, exemplar est deorum iustitiae. "Fabulae nostrae nos docent," inquit sapiens, "deorum potentiam et hominum responsabilitatem."

Lycaon's story, told in Greek and Roman mythology, is an example of the justice of the gods. "Our myths teach us," said a wise man, "about the power of the gods and the responsibility of humans."

Iuppiter et Lycaon, in multis fabulis et artibus, apparuerunt. "Iuppiter et Lycaon," dicit artifex, "in picturis nostris et sculpturis vivunt, nos monentes de virtute et vitiis humanis."

Jupiter and Lycaon have appeared in many stories and artworks. "Jupiter and Lycaon," says an artist, "live in our paintings and sculptures, reminding us of human virtues and vices."

"Lycaon," continuavit artifex, "in lupum mutatus est, sed eius historia nos semper admonet. Potentia et crudelitas sine iustitia et pietate periculosae sunt."

"Lycaon," continued the artist, "was turned into a wolf, but his story always reminds us that power and cruelty without justice and piety are dangerous."

In templis et in libris, fabula de Iove et Lycaone semper narratur. "Haec historia," dicit sacerdos, "nos docet de ira deorum et misericordia. Iuppiter, rex deorum, iustus et potens est."

In temples and books, the story of Jupiter and Lycaon is always told. "This story," says a priest, "teaches us about the wrath and mercy of the gods. Jupiter, king of the gods, is just and powerful."

In silvis Arcadiae, ubi Lycaon rex fuerat, homines nunc deorum mandata meminerunt. "Lycaonis historia," inquit pastor, "nos docet ut iusti et pii simus. Nemo est supra leges deorum."

In the forests of Arcadia, where Lycaon had been king, people now remember the commands of the gods. "Lycaon's story," says a shepherd, "teaches us to be just and pious. No one is above the laws of the gods."

Iuppiter, in caelo sedens, humanitatem observat. "Hominibus secundam chancem dedi," inquit Iuppiter. "Spero eos meliores esse."

Jupiter, sitting in the sky, observes humanity. "I gave humans a second chance," says Jupiter. "I hope they will be better."

Deucalion et Pyrrha, nova humanitas condentes, iustitiam et pietatem docuerunt. "Nova vita nostra," dixit Pyrrha, "exemplum erit futuris generationibus."

Deucalion and Pyrrha, establishing a new humanity, taught justice and piety. "Our new life," said Pyrrha, "will be an example for future generations."

Sic finitur historia de Iove et Lycaone, fabula antiqua plena moribus et monitis. Per eam, antiqui Graeci et Romani de potestate deorum, de iustitia, et de humanitate docti sunt. Haec fabula per saecula manet, docens nos de potentia, responsabilitate, et transformatione.

Thus ends the story of Jupiter and Lycaon, an ancient tale full of morals and lessons. Through it, the ancient Greeks and Romans learned about the power of the gods, justice, and humanity. This story remains through the ages, teaching us about power, responsibility, and transformation.

De Narcisso et Echo

In antiquis temporibus, iuvenis pulcher nomine Narcissus in silvis Graeciae ambulabat.

In ancient times, a handsome young man named Narcissus was walking in the forests of Greece.

Narcissus, clarus pro sua pulchritudine, a multis nymphis et puellis amabatur. Sed Narcissus eas omnes spernebat et solus esse volebat.

Narcissus, famous for his beauty, was loved by many nymphs and girls. But Narcissus rejected them all and wanted to be alone.

"Cur me sequuntur istae nymphae et puellae?" cogitabat Narcissus. "Ego solus esse volo, sine amore et sine molestia."

"Why do these nymphs and girls follow me?" thought Narcissus. "I want to be alone, without love and without bother."

Inter nymphas, erat una loquax et curiosa nomine Echo. Echo, Narcissum videns, statim in amorem eius cecidit. Sed Echo non poterat sua verba incipere, sed solum finire, quia dea Iuno eam sic punierat.

Among the nymphs, there was one talkative and curious nymph named Echo. Seeing Narcissus, Echo immediately fell in love with him. But Echo could not start her own words, only finish them, because the goddess Juno had punished her this way.

Dum Narcissus per silvam ambulabat, "Estne aliquis hic?" clamavit, sonum suae vocis explorans. Echo, prope latens, "Hic!" respondit.

While Narcissus was walking through the forest, he shouted, "Is anyone here?" testing the sound of his voice. Echo, hiding nearby, replied, "Here!"

Narcissus, vocem audiens, miratus est. "Quis est? Veni huc!" clamavit. Echo, gaudio plena, "Huc!" exclamavit et ad Narcissum cucurrit.

Hearing the voice, Narcissus was amazed. "Who is it? Come here!" he shouted. Echo, full of joy, exclaimed, "Here!" and ran to Narcissus.

Sed cum Narcissus Echon vidit, eam repulit. "Manus tuas a me remove! Nolo te!" dixit Narcissus. Echo, tristis et confusa, in silvis sola remansit.

But when Narcissus saw Echo, he rejected her. "Take your hands off me! I don't want you!" said Narcissus. Echo, sad and confused, remained alone in the woods.

"Narcissus crudelis est," flevit Echo. "Eum amo, sed ille me spernit."

"Narcissus is cruel," wept Echo. "I love him, but he scorns me."

Interea, deus iratus, nomine Nemesis, Narcissum pro superbia eius punire voluit. Narcissus ad fontem clarum et tranquillum venit. In aqua suam imaginem vidit et statim in eam amore cecidit.

Meanwhile, an angry god named Nemesis wanted to punish Narcissus for his pride. Narcissus came to a clear and tranquil spring. In the water, he saw his reflection and immediately fell in love with it.

"Quis est iste pulcher iuvenis in aqua?" interrogavit Narcissus. "Eum amo!" Sed non intellegebat se suam imaginem videre.

"Who is this handsome young man in the water?" asked Narcissus. "I love him!" But he did not understand that he was seeing his own reflection.

Narcissus, suae imaginis amore captus, aquam non relinquebat. "Amo te," susurravit Narcissus ad imaginem in aqua. "Sed me tangere non potes."

Narcissus, captivated by the love of his reflection, would not leave the water. "I love you," whispered Narcissus to the image in the water. "But you cannot touch me."

Diuturno tempore, Narcissus ad aquam sedit, suam imaginem contemplans. Tandem, ex amore et desiderio languens, in florem mutatus est.

For a long time, Narcissus sat by the water, gazing at his reflection. At last, weakened by love and longing, he was transformed into a flower.

Narcissus, nunc flos pulcher ad aquae ripam, adhuc eius nomen habet. "Narcissus," inquit viator, "est monitum superbiae et amoris sui."

Narcissus, now a beautiful flower by the water's edge, still bears his name. "Narcissus," says a traveler, "is a warning of pride and self-love."

Echo, in silvis relicta, semper Narcissum amavit, sed eum numquam habuit. Eius vox in montibus et vallibus resonat, semper ultima verba repetens.

Echo, left alone in the woods, always loved Narcissus, but she never had him. Her voice echoes in the mountains and valleys, always repeating the last words.

Sic finitur fabula de Narcisso et Echo, tristis historia amoris unius latere et alterius superbiae. Narcissus, propter amorem sui, in florem mutatus est, et Echo, propter amorem alienum, ad umbras vocis redacta est.

Thus ends the story of Narcissus and Echo, a sad tale of unrequited love on one side and pride on the other. Narcissus, because of his self-love, was turned into a flower, and Echo, because of her unreturned love, was reduced to a mere voice.

"Fabula Narcissi et Echo," dicit magister, "nos docet de periculis amoris sui et negligentiae erga alios. Narcissus tantum de se ipso cogitavit, Echo vero tantum de alio."

"The story of Narcissus and Echo," says the teacher, "teaches us about the dangers of self-love and neglecting others. Narcissus only thought about himself, while Echo only thought about someone else."

In silvis, ubi Narcissus et Echo olim vixerunt, homines adhuc fabulam narrabant. "Videte florem Narcissi," dicunt parentes liberis suis. "Meminisse debemus de aliis curare et non solum de nobis ipsis."

In the forests where Narcissus and Echo once lived, people still tell the story. "Look at the flower of Narcissus," parents say to their children. "We must remember to care for others and not only ourselves."

Echo, licet amissa, per silvas suam tristitiam et amorem resonare pergit. "Echo nos docet," inquit poeta, "amorem verum esse patientem et non possessivum."

Echo, though lost, continues to echo her sadness and love through the woods. "Echo teaches us," says a poet, "that true love is patient and not possessive."

Artes, carmina, et fabulae, historiam Narcissi et Echo saepe celebrant. "In arte nostra," inquit pictor, "Narcissus et Echo vivunt, ut exempla amoris et cautionis."

The arts, poems, and stories often celebrate the story of Narcissus and Echo. "In our art," says a painter, "Narcissus and Echo live as examples of love and caution."

Sic finitur tristis sed docta fabula de Narcisso et Echo. Eorum memoria in cultura et arte per saecula manet, docens nos de amore, superbia, et consequentiis actionum nostrarum.

Thus ends the sad but instructive tale of Narcissus and Echo. Their memory remains in culture and art through the ages, teaching us about love, pride, and the consequences of our actions.

De Cycno et Phaethonte

In antiquis temporibus, post casum Phaethontis, erat iuvenis nomine Cycnus, qui magnopere amicum suum Phaethontem lugens, ad fluminis ripas saepe sedebat.

In ancient times, after the fall of Phaethon, there was a young man named Cycnus, who, greatly mourning his friend Phaethon, often sat by the riverbank.

Cycnus, propter amicitiam profundam cum Phaethonte, corde dolebat.

Cycnus, because of his deep friendship with Phaethon, was heartbroken.

"O Phaethon, amice carissime," saepe murmurabat Cycnus. "Cur tam cito nobis ereptus es? Tuus casus animam meam graviter affligit."

"O Phaethon, dearest friend," Cycnus often murmured. "Why were you taken from us so soon? Your fall gravely burdens my soul."

Cycnus, in ripa fluminis sedens, de amico perdito diu cogitabat. "Ego sine te vivere nescio," dicebat. "Tu mihi plus quam frater fuisti."

Cycnus, sitting by the riverbank, thought long about his lost friend. "I don't know how to live without you," he said. "You were more than a brother to me."

Interim, dei caelestes Cycni maestitiam observabant. Miserti Cycni, deus quidam, "Cycne, tuam maestitiam videmus. Novam vitam tibi donamus," dixit.

Meanwhile, the celestial gods observed Cycnus' sorrow. Moved by his grief, a certain god said, "Cycnus, we see your sadness. We grant you a new life."

Subito, mirum visu, Cycnus in pulchrum cygnum mutatus est. Plumis albis ornatus, Cycnus novam formam admirabat. "Nunc possum volare, et in aquis habitare," dixit Cycnus, mirans novam suam naturam.

Suddenly, in a wondrous sight, Cycnus was transformed into a beautiful swan. Adorned with white feathers, Cycnus marveled at his new form. "Now I can fly, and live in the waters," Cycnus said, amazed at his new nature.

In aquatilibus, Cycnus inter alios cygnos et aves natabat. Sed etiam in hac nova vita, memoria Phaethontis semper cum illo manebat. "Phaethon, semper te in corde meo fero," clamabat Cycnus ad caelum volans.

In the waters, Cycnus swam among other swans and birds. But even in this new life, the memory of Phaethon always stayed with him. "Phaethon, I always carry you in my heart," Cycnus cried as he flew toward the sky.

Cycnus, in aqua natans, dulcem et mitem cantum edebat. Omnes qui eum audiebant, mirabantur. "Cycni cantus nos Phaethontis memoriae admonet," dicebant homines.

Cycnus, swimming in the water, produced a sweet and gentle song. Everyone who heard him was amazed. "The song of the swan reminds us of Phaethon's memory," people would say.

Sed Cycnus non solum propter Phaethontem cantabat, sed etiam propter transformationem suam. "In hoc novo corpore, nova vita mihi data est," cogitabat Cycnus. "Sed amicus meus semper mecum est, in aqua, in aere, et in cantu meo."

But Cycnus sang not only for Phaethon, but also because of his transformation. "In this new body, a new life has been given to me," thought Cycnus. "But my friend is always with me, in the water, in the air, and in my song."

In ripis fluminis, ubi Cycnus natabat, homines saepe veniebant ad eum spectandum. "Videte Cycnum," dicebant. "Ille nos docet de amicitiae vi et de mutationis possibilitate."

On the riverbanks where Cycnus swam, people often came to watch him. "Look at the swan," they would say. "He teaches us about the power of friendship and the possibility of transformation."

"Cycnus, nunc cygnus, semper Phaethontem in corde suo fert," narrabat magister ad discipulos suos. "Etiam in doloribus maximis, vita nova inveniri potest."

"Cycnus, now a swan, always carries Phaethon in his heart," a teacher would tell his students. "Even in the greatest sorrows, a new life can be found."

Tempore, fabula de Cycno et Phaethonte per totam Graeciam narrabatur. "Meminisse debemus," dicebant senes, "quod veri amici numquam obliviscuntur, etiam in novis vitis."

Over time, the tale of Cycnus and Phaethon was told throughout all of Greece. "We must remember," said the elders, "that true friends are never forgotten, even in new lives."

Cycnus, in sua nova forma, per aquas eleganter movebat, semper cantans et Phaethontem memorans. "Cycni cantus," inquit poeta, "est melodia quae nos docet de amoris perpetuitate et spe in maerore."

In his new form, Cycnus moved gracefully through the waters, always singing and remembering Phaethon. "The song of the swan," said the poet, "is a melody that teaches us about the eternity of love and hope in sorrow."

Ita finitur historia de Cycno, qui propter maestitiam in cygnum mutatus est, et quamvis in nova forma, amicitiam et memoriam Phaethontis semper tenuit.

Thus ends the story of Cycnus, who was transformed into a swan because of his grief, and although in a new form, he always kept the friendship and memory of Phaethon.

"In arte nostra," inquit pictor, "Cycnus et Phaethon vivunt, ut exempla fidelitatis et amicitiae verae."

"In our art," says the painter, "Cycnus and Phaethon live on as examples of loyalty and true friendship."

"Fabula Cycni," addit philosophus, "nos docet de naturae transformatione et de vi animi in adversis." In silvis et ad aquas, ubi Cycnus olim vixit, homines fabulam eius narrabant, monentes de amicitiae fortitudine et mutationis potentia.

"The story of Cycnus," adds the philosopher, "teaches us about the transformation of nature and the strength of the spirit in adversity." In the forests and near the waters where Cycnus once lived, people told his story, reminding others of the strength of friendship and the power of transformation.

Parentes ad liberos suos, "Videte cygnum," dicunt. "Est symbolum amicitiae aeternae et mutationis vitae. Cycnus, quamvis mutatus, semper fidelis amico suo mansit."

Parents say to their children, "Look at the swan. It is a symbol of eternal friendship and life's transformation. Cycnus, though changed, always remained faithful to his friend."

Cum sol occidit et luna in caelo apparet, Cycnus adhuc in aqua natat, cantum suavem edens. "Cycni cantus," inquit vates, "nos de amicitiae pulchritudine et de doloris superatione docet."

As the sun sets and the moon appears in the sky, Cycnus still swims in the water, producing a sweet song. "The song of the swan," says the seer, "teaches us about the beauty of friendship and overcoming sorrow."

In theatris et in carminibus, fabula Cycni saepe recitatur. "In fabulis nostris," inquit actor, "Cycnus exemplar est fortitudinis animi et constantiae in amore."

In theaters and poems, the story of Cycnus is often recited. "In our tales," says an actor, "Cycnus is an example of strength of spirit and constancy in love."

Ita per saecula, Cycnus, olim iuvenis, nunc avis, in memoria hominum manet, exemplum praebens amicitiae quae omnia superat.

Thus, through the ages, Cycnus, once a young man, now a bird, remains in the memory of humanity, offering an example of friendship that overcomes all.

"In vita nostra," inquiunt homines, "saepe Cycni similes esse debemus, fortes in adversitate et memores eorum quos amamus."

"In our lives," people say, "we must often be like the swan, strong in adversity and mindful of those we love."

Et sic fabula de Cycno et Phaethonte, historia de amicitia, transformatione, et memoria, in corde et mente hominum per aetatem manet. "Videte cygnum," susurrant venti, "et meminisse de potestate amoris et spe in futurum."

And so the tale of Cycnus and Phaethon, a story of friendship, transformation, and memory, remains in the hearts and minds of people throughout the ages. "Look at the swan," the winds whisper, "and remember the power of love and hope for the future."

De Iove et Callisto

In antiquis temporibus, in silvis Graeciae, erat nympha pulchra nomine Callisto, quae Diana, dea venationis, comitabatur.

In ancient times, in the forests of Greece, there was a beautiful nymph named Callisto, who accompanied Diana, the goddess of the hunt.

Unus dies, Iuppiter, rex deorum, Calliston vidit et eam amavit. Sed sciebat Calliston eum non amaturam esse. Itaque, Iuppiter in formam Dianae se transfiguravit.

One day, Jupiter, king of the gods, saw Callisto and loved her. But he knew that Callisto would not love him. So, Jupiter transformed himself into the form of Diana.

Callisto, Iovem non cognoscens, ad eum accessit. "Diana, cur hic es?" rogavit Callisto. "Venio tecum venari," Iuppiter, ut Diana, respondit.

Callisto, not recognizing Jupiter, approached him. "Diana, why are you here?" Callisto asked. "I have come to hunt with you," Jupiter, in the form of Diana, replied.

Postea, Iuppiter suam veram formam revelavit. Callisto territa et confusa erat. "Iuppiter!" exclamavit. "Quid fecisti?"

Later, Jupiter revealed his true form. Callisto was terrified and confused. "Jupiter!" she exclaimed. "What have you done?"

Iuno, Iovis uxor, de hoc facto irata erat. Iuno Calliston in ursam mutavit. "Nunc forma tua vera monstratur!" clamavit Iuno.

Juno, Jupiter's wife, was angry about this. Juno transformed Callisto into a bear. "Now your true form is revealed!" Juno shouted.

Callisto, nunc ursa, in silvis errabat. Tristis et sola erat, et filium suum, Arcam, desiderabat. Arcas, Callisti filius, erat iuvenis fortis et venator bonus.

Callisto, now a bear, wandered in the woods. She was sad and alone, and she missed her son, Arcas. Arcas, Callisto's son, was a strong young man and a skilled hunter.

Annis post, Arcas in silvis venabat et ursam, matrem suam, vidit. Arcas, matrem non agnoscens, paravit arcum.

Years later, Arcas was hunting in the woods and saw a bear, his mother. Not recognizing her, Arcas prepared his bow.

"Siste!" clamavit deus. "Haec ursa mater tua est!" Arcas, auditis his verbis, consternatus erat.

"Stop!" a god shouted. "This bear is your mother!" Arcas, hearing these words, was shocked.

Dei caelestes miserti sunt et Calliston et Arcam in sidera mutaverunt. Callisto facta est constellatio ursae maioris, et Arcas ursae minoris.

The celestial gods took pity and transformed both Callisto and Arcas into stars. Callisto became the constellation Ursa Major, and Arcas became Ursa Minor.

In caelo, Callisto et Arcas, ut constellationes, semper una sunt. Homines ad caelum spectantes fabulam de Iove, Callisto, et Arca narrabant.

In the sky, Callisto and Arcas, as constellations, are always together. People who looked up at the sky told the story of Jupiter, Callisto, and Arcas.

"Videte stellas," dicebant parentes liberis suis. "Callisto et Arcas nos docent de amore matris et de mutatione vitae."

"Look at the stars," parents would say to their children. "Callisto and Arcas teach us about a mother's love and life's transformations."

Magister ad discipulos suos: "Fabula Callisti," inquit, "nos docet de potestate deorum et de cautione adversus eos. Etiam nos docet de misericordia et spe."

The teacher to his students: "The story of Callisto," he said, "teaches us about the power of the gods and the need for caution toward them. It also teaches us about mercy and hope."

In theatris et in carminibus, historia Callisti et Arcae saepe narrabatur. "In arte nostra," inquit poeta, "Callisto et Arcas vivunt, ut exempla amoris materni et potentiae siderum."

In theaters and poems, the story of Callisto and Arcas was often told. "In our art," said a poet, "Callisto and Arcas live on as examples of maternal love and the power of the stars."

Ita, per saecula, fabula de Callisto, Iove, et Arca, in memoria hominum manebat, narrans de transformatione, de potestate divina, et de vinculo inter matrem et filium. "Meminisse debemus," inquiunt homines, "de amore et protectione. Callisto, quamvis mutata, semper matrem amat."

Thus, through the ages, the tale of Callisto, Jupiter, and Arcas remained in the memory of humanity, telling of transformation, divine power, and the bond between mother and child. "We must remember," people would say, "love and protection. Callisto, though transformed, always loved as a mother."

In silvis, ubi Callisto olim vixit, fabula eius resonabat. "Callisto," inquiunt viatores, "exemplar est matris amoris et sacrificii."

In the forests where Callisto once lived, her story echoed. "Callisto," travelers would say, "is an example of a mother's love and sacrifice."

Nocte, cum caelum stellatum apparet, homines ad sidera Callisti et Arcae spectabant. "In his stellis," inquit astronomus, "historia amoris et mutationis scripta est."

At night, when the starry sky appeared, people would look at the stars of Callisto and Arcas. "In these stars," said an astronomer, "the story of love and transformation is written."

"Fabula Callisti," addit philosophus, "demonstrat nos saepe sub potestate maiorum esse, sed etiam de spe et transformatione narrat." Pueri et puellae, stellas spectantes, de Callisto et Arca somniabant.

"The story of Callisto," adds a philosopher, "shows us that we are often under the power of greater forces, but it also speaks of hope and transformation." Boys and girls, watching the stars, dreamed of Callisto and Arcas.

"Videte ursam in caelo," inquiunt magistri. "Est Callisto, quae nunc stellae sunt. Nos docet ut caute ambulemus et semper amorem in corde teneamus."

"Look at the bear in the sky," the teachers say. "It is Callisto, who is now among the stars. She teaches us to walk carefully and always keep love in our hearts."

Carmen de Callisto et Arca in scholis docebatur. "Cantemus de Callisto," inquiunt discipuli. "Eius fabula nos de fortitudine et amore docet."

A song about Callisto and Arcas was taught in schools. "Let us sing of Callisto," said the students. "Her story teaches us about strength and love."

Et sic, per generationes, fabula de Callisto, Iove, et Arca, in arte, astronomia, et litteris vivebat, monens, docens, et inspirans. "In vita nostra," inquiunt poetae, "Callisto et Arcas nobis viam amoris et spei monstrant."

And so, for generations, the story of Callisto, Jupiter, and Arcas lived on in art, astronomy, and literature, warning, teaching, and inspiring. "In our lives," say poets, "Callisto and Arcas show us the way of love and hope."

In hac fabula antiqua, Callisto et Arcas non solum in sideribus, sed etiam in cordibus et mentibus hominum per aetatem manent, symbola constantiae, amoris, et transformationis in universo mundo. "Memoremus," susurrant stellae, "amorem maternum et potentiam siderum."

In this ancient story, Callisto and Arcas remain not only in the stars but also in the hearts and minds of people throughout the ages, symbols of constancy, love, and transformation in the universe. "Let us remember," whisper the stars, "the power of maternal love and the strength of the stars."

De Corvo et Cornice

In antiquis temporibus, erat corvus qui albas plumas habebat.

In ancient times, there was a raven who had white feathers.

Corvus erat avis Apollinis, dei solis et veritatis. Prope corvum erat cornix, avis prudentiae et sapientiae nota.

The raven was the bird of Apollo, the god of the sun and truth. Near the raven was a crow, known as the bird of wisdom and prudence.

Unus dies, Apollo corvum misit ut custodiret arbores sacras. "Corve," dixit Apollo, "has arbores custodi. Noli sinere ullum malum accidere."

One day, Apollo sent the raven to guard the sacred trees. "Raven," said Apollo, "guard these trees. Do not let any harm come to them."

Corvus, dum in arbore sedebat, vidit arborem plenam pomis dulcibus. Fames corvi magna erat. Itaque, corvus pomum unum comedit. "Apollo non sciet," cogitavit corvus.

The raven, while sitting in the tree, saw a tree full of sweet fruits. The raven was very hungry. So, the raven ate one of the fruits. "Apollo won't know," the raven thought.

Postea, Apollo ad corvum revenit. "Corve, quid factum est? Cur unum pomum deest?" interrogavit Apollo. Corvus, timens poenam, mentitus est. "Non scio," dixit. "Forte avis alia hoc fecit."

Later, Apollo returned to the raven. "Raven, what happened? Why is one fruit missing?" asked Apollo. Fearing punishment, the raven lied. "I don't know," he said. "Perhaps another bird did this."

Cornix, quae prope erat, omnia vidit et audivit. Cornix sapienter dixit, "Corve, noli mentiri. Semper verum dicere melius est."

The crow, who was nearby, saw and heard everything. The crow wisely said, "Raven, do not lie. It is always better to tell the truth."

Apollo, deus sapientiae et potentiae, veritatem scivit. Apollo ad corvum iratus erat. "Corve," dixit Apollo, "quia mentitus es, nunc poenam accipies. Plumae tuae albae nigrae fient."

Apollo, the god of wisdom and power, knew the truth. Apollo was angry at the raven. "Raven," said Apollo, "because you lied, you will now be punished. Your white feathers will turn black."

Subito, plumae corvi mutatae sunt et nigrae factae sunt. Corvus, plumis nigris, tristis erat. "Me paenitet," dixit corvus. "Nunc scio mendacium esse malum."

Suddenly, the raven's feathers changed and became black. The raven, with black feathers, was sad. "I am sorry," said the raven. "Now I know that lying is wrong."

Cornix, ad corvum volans, dixit, "Corve, mendacium semper in malo finitur. Veritatem dicere semper melius est."

The crow, flying over to the raven, said, "Raven, lying always ends badly. It is always better to tell the truth."

Corvus, nunc avis nigra, per silvas et campos volavit, semper de mendacio et poena cogitans. "Nunc intellego," dixit corvus. "Veritas et honestas importantissimae sunt."

The raven, now a black bird, flew through the forests and fields, always thinking about the lie and the punishment. "Now I understand," said the raven. "Truth and honesty are most important."

In villis et urbibus, homines corvum viderunt et de eius plumis nigris mirabantur. "Videte corvum," dicebant. "Ille nos docet de mendacii malo et veritatis virtute."

In villages and cities, people saw the raven and marveled at its black feathers. "Look at the raven," they said. "It teaches us about the evil of lies and the virtue of truth."

Magister ad discipulos suos: "Fabula corvi," inquit, "nos admonet ut semper veraces simus. Mendacium brevis est; veritas aeterna est."

A teacher to his students: "The story of the raven," he said, "reminds us to always be truthful. A lie is short-lived; truth is eternal."

In theatris et in carminibus, historia corvi et cornicis saepe narrabatur. "In arte nostra," inquit poeta, "corvus et cornix vivunt, ut exempla veritatis et sapientiae."

In theaters and poems, the story of the raven and the crow was often told. "In our art," said the poet, "the raven and the crow live on as examples of truth and wisdom."

Per saecula, fabula de corvo et cornice, in memoria hominum manebat, narrans de mendacio, de poena, et de sapientiae valore. "Meminisse debemus," inquiunt homines, "de honestate et integritate."

For centuries, the story of the raven and the crow remained in the memory of people, telling of lies, punishment, and the value of wisdom. "We must remember," people say, "about honesty and integrity."

In silvis, ubi corvus et cornix olim vixerunt, fabula eorum resonabat. "Corvus," inquiunt viatores, "exemplar est mendacii poenae. Cornix, contra, sapientiae et honestatis."

In the forests where the raven and crow once lived, their story echoed. "The raven," travelers said, "is an example of the punishment for lies. The crow, on the other hand, is an example of wisdom and honesty."

Nocte, cum corvus et cornix in ramis arborum dormiebant, homines ad stellas spectabant et de eorum fabula cogitabant. "In his avibus," inquit astronomus, "historia moralis scripta est."

At night, when the raven and the crow slept in the branches of the trees, people would look at the stars and think about their story. "In these birds," said an astronomer, "a moral story is written."

"Fabula corvi et cornicis," addit philosophus, "demonstrat nos sub potestate veritatis esse, et mendacium semper in malo finire." Pueri et puellae, aves in caelo volantes spectantes, de corvo et cornice somniabant.

"The story of the raven and the crow," adds a philosopher, "shows that we are under the power of truth, and that lies always end in harm." Boys and girls, watching the birds flying in the sky, dreamed of the raven and the crow.

"Videte aves," inquiunt magistri. "Sunt symbola veritatis et falsitatis. Corvus, quamvis mutatus, semper mendacii monitum fert."

"Look at the birds," the teachers say. "They are symbols of truth and falsehood. The raven, though transformed, always carries a warning about lying."

Carmen de corvo et cornice in scholis docebatur. "Cantemus de corvo," inquiunt discipuli. "Eius fabula nos de veritate et mendacio docet."

A song about the raven and the crow was taught in schools. "Let us sing about the raven," said the students. "His story teaches us about truth and lies."

Et sic, per generationes, fabula de corvo albo, qui propter mendacium niger factus est, et de cornice sapiente in arte, litteris, et cultura vivebat, monens, docens, et inspirans. "In vita nostra," inquiunt poetae, "corvus et cornix nobis viam honestatis et sapientiae monstrant."

And so, through generations, the story of the white raven, who was turned black because of a lie, and of the wise crow lived on in art, literature, and culture, warning, teaching, and inspiring. "In our lives," poets say, "the raven and the crow show us the way of honesty and wisdom."

In hac fabula antiqua, corvus et cornix non solum in silvis et campis, sed etiam in cordibus et mentibus hominum per aetatem manent, symbola mendacii consequentiarum et sapientiae virtutis. "Memoremus," susurrant venti, "veritatem semper praestare et mendacium vitare."

In this ancient tale, the raven and the crow remain not only in the forests and fields but also in the hearts and minds of people throughout the ages, symbols of the consequences of lies and the virtue of wisdom. "Let us remember," the winds whisper, "that truth always prevails and lies should be avoided."

De Ocyrhoe

In antiquis temporibus, in silvis Graeciae, erat nympha nomine Ocyrhoe.

In ancient times, in the forests of Greece, there was a nymph named Ocyrhoe.

Ocyrhoe, filia Chironis, centauri sapientis et medici, erat pulchra et studiosa.

Ocyrhoe, the daughter of Chiron, the wise centaur and healer, was beautiful and studious.

Unus dies, Ocyrhoe donum prophetiae accepit. Poterat futura videre et multa scire quae alii ignorabant. "Mirabile donum est," cogitavit Ocyrhoe. "Nunc possum futura praedicere."

One day, Ocyrhoe received the gift of prophecy. She could see the future and knew many things that others did not. "This is a wonderful gift," thought Ocyrhoe. "Now I can predict the future."

Ocyrhoe de Aesculapio, filio Apollinis et medico futuro, prophetavit. "Aesculapius, magnus medicus eris," dixit Ocyrhoe. "Mortuos vitam dabis et multi te laudabunt."

Ocyrhoe prophesied about Aesculapius, the future physician and son of Apollo. "Aesculapius, you will be a great healer," said Ocyrhoe. "You will give life to the dead, and many will praise you."

Sed dei, Apollinis in primis, de Ocyrhoes prophetiis irati sunt. "Nymphae non debent futura scire," dixerunt. "Hoc contra leges deorum est."

But the gods, especially Apollo, were angry about Ocyrhoe's prophecies. "Nymphs should not know the future," they said. "This is against the laws of the gods."

Itaque, dei Ocyrhoen punire statuerunt. "Quia futura praedixisti, nunc in formam aliam mutaberis," dixerunt dei. Et subito, Ocyrhoe in equam, id est feminam equi, mutata est.

So, the gods decided to punish Ocyrhoe. "Because you predicted the future, you will now be transformed into another form," said the gods. And suddenly, Ocyrhoe was changed into a mare, that is, a female horse.

Ocyrhoe, nunc equa, tristis et confusa erat. "Cur me sic punistis?" clamavit Ocyrhoe. "Donum meum uti volui ad bonum."

Ocyrhoe, now a mare, was sad and confused. "Why have you punished me like this?" cried Ocyrhoe. "I wanted to use my gift for good."

In silvis, Ocyrhoe, nunc equa, errabat. Homines et aliae nymphae eam videbant et de eius mutatione mirabantur. "Videte Ocyrhoen," dicebant. "Erat nympha, nunc est equa."

In the woods, Ocyrhoe, now a mare, wandered. People and other nymphs saw her and marveled at her transformation. "Look at Ocyrhoe," they said. "She was a nymph, now she is a mare."

Magister ad discipulos suos: "Fabula Ocyrhoes," inquit, "nos docet de limitibus nostris et de humilitate. Non semper omnia scire possumus, et non semper omnia debemus."

A teacher to his students: "The story of Ocyrhoe," he said, "teaches us about our limits and humility. We cannot always know everything, and we should not always try."

In theatris et in carminibus, historia Ocyrhoes saepe narrabatur. "In arte nostra," inquit poeta, "Ocyrhoe vivit, ut exemplum sapientiae et cautionis."

In theaters and poems, the story of Ocyrhoe was often told. "In our art," said a poet, "Ocyrhoe lives on as an example of wisdom and caution."

Per saecula, fabula de Ocyrhoe, nympha quae in equam mutata est propter suam prophetiam, in memoria hominum manebat, narrans de potentia scientiae et de periculis superbiae. "Meminisse debemus," inquiunt homines, "de modestia et prudentia."

For centuries, the story of Ocyrhoe, the nymph who was transformed into a mare because of her prophecy, remained in people's memory, telling of the power of knowledge and the dangers of pride. "We must remember," people say, "to be humble and wise."

In silvis, ubi Ocyrhoe olim vixit, fabula eius resonabat. "Ocyrhoe," inquiunt viatores, "exemplar est curiositatis et poenae. Dei, interdum, dona dant et tollunt."

In the woods where Ocyrhoe once lived, her story echoed. "Ocyrhoe," travelers say, "is an example of curiosity and punishment. The gods sometimes give gifts and take them away."

Nocte, cum stellae in caelo micant, homines ad caelum spectabant et de Ocyrhoe cogitabant. "In his stellis," inquit astronomus, "historia cautionis et sapientiae scripta est."

At night, when the stars twinkled in the sky, people would look up and think of Ocyrhoe. "In these stars," said an astronomer, "a story of caution and wisdom is written."

"Fabula Ocyrhoes," addit philosophus, "demonstrat nos sub potestate maiorum esse, et dona nostra cum cautione uti debemus." Pueri et puellae, equum in campo spectantes, de Ocyrhoe somniabant.

"The story of Ocyrhoe," adds a philosopher, "shows us that we are under the power of greater forces, and we must use our gifts with caution." Boys and girls, watching a horse in the field, dreamed of Ocyrhoe.

"Videte equam," inquiunt magistri. "Est Ocyrhoe, quae propter suam scientiam et audaciam mutata est. Nos docet ut dona nostra sapienter utamur."

"Look at the mare," teachers say. "It is Ocyrhoe, who was changed because of her knowledge and daring. She teaches us to use our gifts wisely."

Carmen de Ocyrhoe in scholis docebatur. "Cantemus de Ocyrhoe," inquiunt discipuli. "Eius fabula nos de limitibus et respectu deorum docet."

A song about Ocyrhoe was taught in schools. "Let us sing about Ocyrhoe," the students say. "Her story teaches us about limits and respect for the gods."

Et sic, per generationes, fabula de Ocyrhoe, nympha quae donum prophetiae habuit et propter hoc in equam mutata est, in arte, litteris, et cultura vivebat, monens, docens, et inspirans. "In vita nostra," inquiunt poetae, "Ocyrhoe nobis viam sapientiae et modestiae monstrat."

And so, for generations, the story of Ocyrhoe, the nymph who had the gift of prophecy and was transformed into a mare because of it, lived on in art, literature, and culture, warning, teaching, and inspiring. "In our lives," say poets, "Ocyrhoe shows us the way of wisdom and humility."

In hac fabula antiqua, Ocyrhoe non solum in silvis et campis, sed etiam in cordibus et mentibus hominum per aetatem manet, symbola scientiae limitum et humilitatis. "Memoremus," susurrant venti, "sapientiam esse donum, sed cum humilitate et cautione utendum."

In this ancient story, Ocyrhoe remains not only in the forests and fields but also in the hearts and minds of people throughout the ages, a symbol of the limits of knowledge and humility. "Let us remember," whisper the winds, "that wisdom is a gift, but it must be used with humility and caution."

In caelo, ubi stellae lucem suam spargunt, fabula de Ocyrhoe, nympha quae in equam mutata est, memoriam de potentia et limite scientiae, de prudentia in donis utendis, et de respectu erga potestates superiores servat. "In stellis," inquiunt astronomi, "Ocyrhoe nos de sapientia et vita docet."

In the sky, where the stars spread their light, the story of Ocyrhoe, the nymph who was turned into a mare, preserves the memory of the power and limits of knowledge, the wisdom in using gifts, and respect for higher powers. "In the stars," say astronomers, "Ocyrhoe teaches us about wisdom and life."

De Batto et Mercurio

In antiquis temporibus, Mercurius, deus nuntiorum et furum, audax consilium cepit.

In ancient times, Mercury, the god of messengers and thieves, made a bold decision.

Apollinis boves furatus est. Mercurius, astutus et callidus, boves in locum secretum duxit.

He stole Apollo's cattle. Mercury, clever and cunning, led the cattle to a secret place.

Erat homo in illa regione nomine Battus. Battus erat pastor et terram suam diligenter custodiebat. Die illo, Battus Mercurium vidit cum bovibus Apollinis. "Quis est ille?" cogitavit Battus. "Cur boves Apollinis ducit?"

There was a man in that region named Battus. Battus was a shepherd who guarded his land carefully. That day, Battus saw Mercury with Apollo's cattle. "Who is that?" thought Battus. "Why is he leading Apollo's cattle?"

Mercurius, Battum videntem, timuit ne furtum suum revelaretur. Itaque, ad Batton accessit. "Salve, Batte," dixit Mercurius. "Secretum tibi habeo."

Mercury, seeing Battus, feared that his theft would be revealed. So, he approached Battus. "Greetings, Battus," said Mercury. "I have a secret for you."

Battus, Mercurium agnoscentem, admiratus est. "Mercuri, cur hic es? Et cur boves Apollinis habes?" interrogavit Battus.

Battus, recognizing Mercury, was amazed. "Mercury, why are you here? And why do you have Apollo's cattle?" asked Battus.

Mercurius, callide respondit, "Batte, haec res secreta est. Te oro, ne cui dicas quod vidisti. Tibi donum dabo si taces."

Mercury replied cleverly, "Battus, this is a secret matter. I beg you not to tell anyone what you saw. I will give you a gift if you remain silent."

Battus, dono promisso laetus, respondit, "Mercuri, tibi promitto. Secretum tuum servabo. Nemo sciet de bovibus."

Battus, happy with the promise of a gift, replied, "Mercury, I promise you. I will keep your secret. No one will know about the cattle."

Mercurius, tamen, Batto non confidebat. Post paululum, Mercurius se in alium hominem transformavit et ad Batton rediit. "Salve," dixit Mercurius, "audivi de furto bovum. Scisne quis boves furatus sit?"

However, Mercury did not trust Battus. After a little while, Mercury transformed himself into another man and returned to Battus. "Greetings," said Mercury, "I heard about the theft of the cattle. Do you know who stole them?"

Battus, Mercurium non agnoscens, cito respondit, "Ego scio! Mercurius, deus, boves furatus est!" Mercurius, sua vera forma revelata, iratus erat.

Battus, not recognizing Mercury, quickly replied, "I know! Mercury, the god, stole the cattle!" Mercury, revealing his true form, was furious.

"Batte, mihi promisisti!" exclamavit Mercurius. "Nunc proditionem tuam puniam." Et subito, Battus in saxum mutatus est.

"Battus, you promised me!" exclaimed Mercury. "Now I will punish your betrayal." And suddenly, Battus was transformed into a stone.

Saxum Battum factum, in campo stetit, monumentum hominis qui promissum fregit. Homines et dii de Batto et Mercurio fabulam narrabant.

The stone that Battus became stood in the field, a monument to the man who broke his promise. People and gods told the story of Battus and Mercury.

"Videte saxum," dicebant parentes liberis suis. "Est Battus, qui non fidem servavit. Nos docet ut promissa nostra custodiamus."

"Look at the stone," parents would tell their children. "That is Battus, who did not keep his word. It teaches us to keep our promises."

Magister ad discipulos suos: "Fabula Batto et Mercurio," inquit, "nos admonet ut veraces simus. Fides et honestas importantissimae sunt."

A teacher to his students: "The story of Battus and Mercury," he said, "reminds us to be truthful. Trust and honesty are most important."

In theatris et in carminibus, historia Batto et Mercurio saepe narrabatur. "In arte nostra," inquit poeta, "Battus et Mercurius vivunt, ut exempla fidelitatis et cautionis."

In theaters and poems, the story of Battus and Mercury was often told. "In our art," said a poet, "Battus and Mercury live on as examples of loyalty and caution."

Per saecula, fabula de Batto, qui propter proditionem in saxum mutatus est, et de Mercurio, deo astuto, in memoria hominum manebat, narrans de fide, de mendacio, et de iustitiae poena. "Meminisse debemus," inquiunt homines, "promissionem semper servare et veritatem dicere."

For centuries, the story of Battus, who was turned into a stone because of his betrayal, and of Mercury, the cunning god, remained in people's memory, telling of faith, lies, and the punishment of justice. "We must remember," people say, "to always keep promises and tell the truth."

In regione, ubi Battus olim vixit, fabula eius resonabat. "Battus," inquiunt viatores, "exemplar est mendacii consequentiarum. Promissionem fregit et poenam accepit."

In the region where Battus once lived, his story echoed. "Battus," travelers say, "is an example of the consequences of lies. He broke his promise and received his punishment."

Nocte, cum stellae in caelo micant, homines ad caelum spectabant et de Batto et Mercurio cogitabant. "In his stellis," inquit astronomus, "historia moralis scripta est."

At night, when the stars twinkled in the sky, people looked up and thought of Battus and Mercury. "In these stars," said an astronomer, "a moral story is written."

"Fabula Batto et Mercurio," addit philosophus, "demonstrat nos sub potestate veritatis esse, et mendacium semper in malo finire." Pueri et puellae, saxum in campo spectantes, de Batto et Mercurio somniabant.

"The story of Battus and Mercury," adds a philosopher, "shows us that we are under the power of truth, and that lies always end badly." Boys and girls, watching the stone in the field, dreamed of Battus and Mercury.

"Videte saxum," inquiunt magistri. "Est Battus, qui propter mendacium saxum factus est. Nos docet ne promissa nostra frangamus."

"Look at the stone," teachers say. "It is Battus, who was turned into a stone because of a lie. He teaches us not to break our promises."

Carmen de Batto et Mercurio in scholis docebatur. "Cantemus de Batto," inquiunt discipuli. "Eius fabula nos de honestate et poena mendacii docet."

A song about Battus and Mercury was taught in schools. "Let us sing about Battus," said the students. "His story teaches us about honesty and the punishment of lies."

Et sic, per generationes, fabula de Batto, qui propter mendacium et proditionem in saxum mutatus est, et de Mercurio, deo callido, in arte, litteris, et cultura vivebat, monens, docens, et inspirans. "In vita nostra," inquiunt poetae, "Battus et Mercurius nobis viam honestatis et fidei monstrant."

And so, through generations, the story of Battus, who was turned into a stone because of lies and betrayal, and of Mercury, the clever god, lived on in art, literature, and culture, warning, teaching, and inspiring. "In our lives," say poets, "Battus and Mercury show us the way of honesty and trust."

In hac fabula antiqua, Battus et Mercurius non solum in campis et silvis, sed etiam in cordibus et mentibus hominum per aetatem manent, symbola mendacii et fidelitatis, monentes nos de importantia promissionum servandarum et de periculis mendacii. "Memoremus," susurrant venti, "veritatem et fidem in omni vita nostra servare."

In this ancient story, Battus and Mercury remain not only in the fields and forests but also in the hearts and minds of people through the ages, symbols of lies and loyalty, reminding us of the importance of keeping promises and the dangers of deceit. "Let us remember," whisper the winds, "to always keep truth and faith in our lives."

De Aglauro et Mercurio

In antiquis temporibus Athenis, erat puella nomine Herse, quae erat pulchra et amabilis.

In ancient times in Athens, there was a girl named Herse, who was beautiful and kind.

Mercurius, deus nuntiorum et furum, Hersen vidit et statim in eam amore cecidit.

Mercury, the god of messengers and thieves, saw Herse and immediately fell in love with her.

"Herse pulcherrima est," cogitavit Mercurius. "Eam amare non possum resistere." Itaque Mercurius ad domum Hersis venit ut amorem suum confiteretur.

"Herse is very beautiful," thought Mercury. "I cannot resist loving her." So Mercury went to Herse's home to confess his love.

Sed Aglauros, soror Hersis, in via stetit et Hersem Mercuriumque convenire non sinebat. "Cur hic es, Mercuri?" interrogavit Aglauros.

But Aglauros, Herse's sister, stood in the way and did not allow Mercury to meet with Herse. "Why are you here, Mercury?" Aglauros asked.

Mercurius Aglaurum videns, respondit: "Veni ad Hersem videre. Eam amo et cum ea loqui volo." Aglauros tamen Mercurium non sinebat.

Mercury, seeing Aglauros, replied, "I came to see Herse. I love her and want to speak with her." However, Aglauros would not allow Mercury to pass.

Aglauros invidia plena erat, videbat enim Hersem a deo amari et hoc ei non placebat. "Cur Herse? Cur non ego?" cogitavit Aglauros.

Aglauros was full of envy because she saw that Herse was loved by a god, and this displeased her. "Why Herse? Why not me?" thought Aglauros.

Mercurius, iratus et frustratus, poenam Aglaurae imponere statuit. "Aglauro," dixit Mercurius, "quia me prohibes, nunc poenas dabis."

Mercury, angry and frustrated, decided to punish Aglauros. "Aglauros," said Mercury, "because you are blocking me, you will now pay the price."

Et subito, Mercurius magia sua Aglauram in saxum mutavit. Aglauros, nunc saxum, movere non potuit. "Me paenitet," susurravit Aglauros, sed iam sero erat.

And suddenly, Mercury, using his magic, turned Aglauros into stone. Aglauros, now a stone, could no longer move. "I am sorry," whispered Aglauros, but it was already too late.

Homines Athenienses, Aglauros saxum videntes, mirabantur. "Videte Aglauros," dicebant. "Ea invidia et obstinatione poenas dedit."

The Athenians, seeing Aglauros as a stone, were amazed. "Look at Aglauros," they said. "She paid the price for her envy and stubbornness."

Magister ad discipulos suos: "Fabula Aglauros," inquit, "nos docet de periculis invidiae et superbiae. Invidia nos ad malum ducit."

A teacher to his students: "The story of Aglauros," he said, "teaches us about the dangers of envy and pride. Envy leads us to harm."

In theatris et in carminibus, historia Aglauros et Mercurii saepe narrabatur. "In arte nostra," inquit poeta, "Aglauros et Mercurius vivunt, ut exempla cautionis et amoris."

In theaters and poems, the story of Aglauros and Mercury was often told. "In our art," said a poet, "Aglauros and Mercury live on as examples of caution and love."

Per saecula, fabula de Aglauro, quae propter invidiam et obstinationem in saxum mutata est, et de Mercurio, deo amoris et astutiae, in memoria hominum manebat, narrans de passionibus humanis et de poenis divinis. "Meminisse debemus," inquiunt homines, "moderationem et humilitatem."

For centuries, the story of Aglauros, who was turned into stone because of envy and stubbornness, and of Mercury, the god of love and cleverness, remained in people's memory, telling of human passions and divine punishments. "We must remember," people say, "moderation and humility."

In Athenis, ubi Aglauros olim vixit, fabula eius resonabat. "Aglauros," inquiunt viatores, "exemplar est invidiae et eius consequentiarum. Dei, interdum, nos in vias iustitiae ducunt."

In Athens, where Aglauros once lived, her story echoed. "Aglauros," travelers say, "is an example of envy and its consequences. The gods sometimes guide us toward justice."

Nocte, cum stellae in caelo micant, homines ad caelum spectabant et de Aglauro et Mercurio cogitabant. "In his stellis," inquit astronomus, "historia invidiae et amoris scripta est."

At night, when the stars twinkled in the sky, people looked up and thought about Aglauros and Mercury. "In these stars," said an astronomer, "the story of envy and love is written."

"Fabula Aglauros et Mercurii," addit philosophus, "demonstrat nos sub potestate maioribus esse, et invidia et obstinatio semper in malo finiunt." Pueri et puellae, saxum in agro spectantes, de Aglauro et Mercurio somniabant.

"The story of Aglauros and Mercury," adds a philosopher, "shows us that we are under the power of greater forces, and envy and stubbornness always end badly." Boys and girls, watching the stone in the field, dreamed of Aglauros and Mercury.

"Videte saxum," inquiunt magistri. "Est Aglauros, quae propter invidiam et obstinationem saxum facta est. Nos docet ne invidiamus et ne obstinemus."

"Look at the stone," teachers say. "It is Aglauros, who was turned into a stone because of envy and stubbornness. She teaches us not to be envious and not to be obstinate."

Carmen de Aglauro et Mercurio in scholis docebatur. "Cantemus de Aglauro," inquiunt discipuli. "Eius fabula nos de periculis invidiae et amoris non recti docet."

A song about Aglauros and Mercury was taught in schools. "Let us sing of Aglauros," said the students. "Her story teaches us about the dangers of envy and misguided love."

Et sic, per generationes, fabula de Aglauro, quae propter invidiam et obstinationem in saxum mutata est, et de Mercurio, deo amoris et calliditatis, in arte, litteris, et cultura vivebat, monens, docens, et inspirans. "In vita nostra," inquiunt poetae, "Aglauros et Mercurius nobis viam prudentiae et amoris recti monstrant."

And so, through generations, the story of Aglauros, who was turned into a stone because of envy and stubbornness, and of Mercury, the god of love and cleverness, lived on in art, literature, and culture, warning, teaching, and inspiring. "In our lives," poets say, "Aglauros and Mercury show us the way of wisdom and proper love."

In hac fabula antiqua, Aglauros et Mercurius non solum in Athenis et campis, sed etiam in cordibus et mentibus hominum per aetatem manent, symbola passionum humanarum et sapientiae divinae. "Memoremus," susurrant venti, "amorem verum et sincerum sequi et invidiam vitare."

In this ancient story, Aglauros and Mercury remain not only in Athens and the fields but also in the hearts and minds of people throughout the ages, symbols of human passions and divine wisdom. "Let us remember," the winds whisper, "to follow true and sincere love and to avoid envy."

In Athenis, ubi templum Mercurii et saxum Aglauros stant, fabula de Aglauro, quae amore et invidia mota est, et de Mercurio, qui passionem et sapientiam repraesentat, historiam de humanis affectibus, divina iustitia, et amoris potestate narrat. "In templis et saxo," inquiunt sacerdotes, "Aglauros et Mercurius nos de vita, amore, et iustitia docent."

In Athens, where Mercury's temple and Aglauros's stone stand, the story of Aglauros, driven by love and envy, and of Mercury, who represents passion and wisdom, tells the tale of human emotions, divine justice, and the power of love. "In the temples and the stone," say the priests, "Aglauros and Mercury teach us about life, love, and justice."

De Semele et Dionyso

Olim in Thebis, Semele, Cadmi filia, erat.

Once in Thebes, there was Semele, the daughter of Cadmus.

Pulchra et omnibus grata, deorum quoque animos movebat. Maxime Iuppiter, deorum rex, in Semelem incidit et eam amare coepit.

Beautiful and beloved by all, she also stirred the hearts of the gods. Most of all, Jupiter, the king of the gods, fell for Semele and began to love her.

Semele, Iovis amoris ignara, vitam suam in Thebis agebat. Interea, Iuno, Iovis uxor, de mariti amore irata erat. "Cur Semele? Cur non ego?" saepe cogitabat.

Semele, unaware of Jupiter's love, lived her life in Thebes. Meanwhile, Juno, Jupiter's wife, was angry about her husband's love. "Why Semele? Why not me?" she often thought.

Iuppiter, saepe ad Semelem veniens, semper sub alia forma apparebat. Semele gaudebat, sed aliquando dubitabat. "Si vere me amas," Semele Iovi dixit, "te in vera forma mihi ostende."

Jupiter, often visiting Semele, always appeared in another form. Semele was happy, but sometimes she doubted. "If you truly love me," Semele said to Jupiter, "show yourself to me in your true form."

Iuno, hoc audito, consilium cepit. In formam aniculae se mutavit et ad Semelem venit. "Si deus est," Iuno, ut anicula, dixit, "iube eum se in vera forma tibi apparere."

Juno, hearing this, devised a plan. She transformed into an old woman and went to Semele. "If he is truly a god," Juno, in the form of an old woman, said, "order him to appear to you in his true form."

Semele, consilio Iunonis capta, Iovem iterum rogavit. "Si me amas," dixit, "in tua vera forma veni." Iuppiter, promissis obstrictus, tristis erat. "Heu," dixit, "hoc periculosum est."

Semele, deceived by Juno's advice, asked Jupiter again. "If you love me," she said, "come to me in your true form." Jupiter, bound by his promises, was sad. "Alas," he said, "this is dangerous."

Tamen, Iuppiter promissum servavit. Fulmine cinctus ad Semelem venit. Semele, Iovis veram potentiam non ferens, igne consumpta est. Iuppiter, maestus, ex cineribus filium servavit.

However, Jupiter kept his promise. Surrounded by lightning, he came to Semele. Semele, unable to bear Jupiter's true power, was consumed by fire. Jupiter, grieving, saved their son from the ashes.

Filius erat Dionysus, postea deus vini et festivitatis. Iuppiter, Dionysum protegens, eum in immortalem fecit. Dionysus in Olympo apud alios deos educatus est.

The son was Dionysus, who later became the god of wine and festivity. Protecting Dionysus, Jupiter made him immortal. Dionysus was raised in Olympus among the other gods.

Dionysus adultus, per Graeciam iter fecit. Ubique, hominibus vinum et festivitatem docebat. "Gaudete et celebrate," Dionysus dicebat.

As an adult, Dionysus traveled through Greece. Everywhere, he taught people about wine and festivity. "Rejoice and celebrate," Dionysus would say.

Cultus Dionysi per terras diffusus est. Homines Bacchum, alterum Dionysi nomen, laudabant. Dionysus, per vias et montes vagans, multa mirabilia fecit.

The worship of Dionysus spread across the lands. People praised Bacchus, another name for Dionysus. Dionysus, wandering through roads and mountains, performed many wonders.

Interdum, Dionysus monstra magna vicit. Semper, homines eum deum potentem et laetum colebant. Sed Dionysus non solum laetitia, sed etiam furor erat. Qui Dionysum non coluerunt, saepe poenas dabant.

At times, Dionysus defeated great monsters. Always, people worshipped him as a powerful and joyful god. But Dionysus was not only joy, he was also fury. Those who did not worship Dionysus often paid a price.

Fabula Dionysi de vita, morte, et renascentia est. Dionysus, inter mortales et deos versans, exemplum potentiae divinae et transformationis est.

The story of Dionysus is about life, death, and rebirth. Dionysus, moving between mortals and gods, is an example of divine power and transformation.

Semele, mater Dionysi, semper in memoria hominum manet. "De amoribus deorum et mortalium," senes narrabant, "saepe mirabilia et terribilia fiunt."

Semele, the mother of Dionysus, always remains in the memory of people. "In the loves of gods and mortals," elders would tell, "wonders and terrible things often happen."

Dionysus, per Graeciam iter faciens, semper matrem suam in mente habebat. "Matris meae memoria me movet," Dionysus dicebat. "Eius historia me docet de amoris potentia et periculis."

Dionysus, traveling through Greece, always kept his mother in mind. "The memory of my mother moves me," Dionysus would say. "Her story teaches me about the power and dangers of love."

De Tiresia

Olim in Thebis vivebat Tiresias, vates clarus.

Once in Thebes lived Tiresias, a famous prophet.

Tiresias, vaticinationis arte praeditus, in rebus mirabilibus versabatur. Eius vita tamen non semper tranquilla erat.

Tiresias, endowed with the art of prophecy, was involved in extraordinary matters. However, his life was not always peaceful.

Quadam die, dum in silva ambulabat, Tiresias serpentes inter se pugnantes vidit. Eos baculo percussit et, mirum in modum, in feminam mutatus est.

One day, while walking in the forest, Tiresias saw two snakes fighting. He struck them with his staff and, miraculously, was transformed into a woman.

Tiresias, nova forma perterritus, tamen novam vitam coepit.

Tiresias, frightened by this new form, nevertheless began a new life.

Septem annos ut femina vixit. Deinde, iterum serpentes vidit et in virum rursus mutatus est. Vita Tiresiae mirabilibus plena erat.

For seven years, he lived as a woman. Then, he saw the snakes again and was transformed back into a man. Tiresias' life was full of wonders.

De sexuum voluptatibus inter Iovem et Iunonem contentio orta est. "Quis magis fruatur, vir an femina?" interrogavit Iuppiter. "Femina," respondit Iuno.

A dispute arose between Jupiter and Juno about the pleasures of the sexes. "Who enjoys more, man or woman?" asked Jupiter. "The woman," replied Juno.

Ad Tiresiam Iuppiter et Iuno accesserunt. "Tu, qui uterque sexus fuisti, responde," dixit Iuppiter. Tiresias, paululum dubitans, tandem respondit, "Vir minus fruitur."

Jupiter and Juno went to Tiresias. "You, who have been both sexes, answer," said Jupiter. Tiresias, hesitating a little, finally responded, "The man enjoys less."

Iuno, irata Tiresiae sententia, visum ei ademit. Tiresias, caecus factus, tamen tranquillitatem servavit. Iuppiter, visum eripiens, donum vaticinationis ei concessit.

Juno, angry at Tiresias' answer, took away his sight. Tiresias, made blind, still remained calm. Jupiter, taking away his sight, granted him the gift of prophecy.

Tiresias, caecus sed vates, multa futura praedixit. Thebanis consilium saepe dabat et multos adiuvabat. Fama eius per Graeciam crescebat.

Tiresias, blind but a prophet, predicted many futures. He often gave advice to the Thebans and helped many people. His fame grew throughout Greece.

Oedipus, rex Thebarum, quoque ad Tiresiam venit. "O Tiresia, fata mea narra," rogavit Oedipus. Tiresias, veritatem sciens, regi respondit.

Oedipus, king of Thebes, also came to Tiresias. "Oh Tiresias, tell me my fate," Oedipus asked. Tiresias, knowing the truth, responded to the king.

Tiresias, annis plenus, multa vidit et multos monuit. Vita eius exemplar erat fatorum et deorum voluntatis. Saepe in oraculis et fabulis memorabatur.

Tiresias, full of years, saw many things and warned many people. His life was an example of fate and the will of the gods. He was often remembered in oracles and stories.

Morte Tiresiae, Thebani eum magnis honoribus sepelierunt. "Tiresias, vates noster, semper in memoria tenetur," dicebant.

At Tiresias' death, the Thebans buried him with great honors. "Tiresias, our prophet, will always be remembered," they said.

Tiresiae historia de transformatione et perceptione est. Eius vita docet nos de rebus invisibilibus et internis. Tiresias, etiam caecus, plura quam ceteri videbat.

The story of Tiresias is one of transformation and perception. His life teaches us about things unseen and internal. Tiresias, even blind, saw more than others.

In mythologia Graeca, Tiresias magna momenti persona est. Eius fabulae adhuc narrantur, docentes nos de vita, fato, et sapientia.

In Greek mythology, Tiresias is a figure of great importance. His stories are still told, teaching us about life, fate, and wisdom.

De Pentheo et Baccho

Pentheus, Thebarum rex, erat vir severus et superbus.

Pentheus, the king of Thebes, was a stern and proud man.

Dionysi, dei vini et festivitatis, sacra neglegebat. "Non est locus his festis in Thebis," Pentheus dicebat.

He neglected the sacred rites of Dionysus, the god of wine and festivity. "There is no place for these festivals in Thebes," Pentheus would say.

Bacchus, deus vini, hoc audivit et statuit Thebas adire. Bacchus, deus potens et mysticus, in urbem intravit. Multos Thebanos ad cultum suum traxit, festa et cantus afferens.

Bacchus, the god of wine, heard this and decided to visit Thebes. Bacchus, a powerful and mystical god, entered the city. He attracted many Thebans to his cult, bringing festivals and songs.

Pentheus, Bacchum videntes, iratus est. "Bacchum captivabo!" inquit. Sed Bacchus, non tam facile capiendus, Pentheum fefellit.

Pentheus, seeing Bacchus, became angry. "I will capture Bacchus!" he said. But Bacchus, not so easily caught, tricked Pentheus.

Bacchus Pentheo visiones falsas ostendit. Pentheus, hallucinationibus captus, in montem ascendit. Putabat se Bacchum et eius sectatores ibi invenire.

Bacchus showed Pentheus false visions. Captivated by hallucinations, Pentheus climbed the mountain. He thought he would find Bacchus and his followers there.

Agave, mater Penthei, et aliae mulieres, Bacchi sacris deditae, ad montem venerunt. Bacchus eas furore implevit. Agave et ceterae, non se ipsas agnoscentes, in Pentheum impetum fecerunt.

Agave, the mother of Pentheus, and other women devoted to the rites of Bacchus came to the mountain. Bacchus filled them with frenzy. Agave and the others, not recognizing themselves, attacked Pentheus.

Pentheus, a sua matre et amicis discerptus est. Agave, caput filii gerens, ad urbem rediit. In urbe, Agave caput Penthei ostendit, adhuc furore captata.

Pentheus was torn apart by his mother and her friends. Agave, carrying the head of her son, returned to the city. In the city, Agave displayed Pentheus's head, still caught in her frenzy.

Cum furore recessit, Agave horrendam veritatem agnovit. "Heu, fili mi!" exclamavit. "Quid feci?" Thebani, hoc videntes, tristitia et horrore capti sunt.

When the frenzy subsided, Agave realized the horrifying truth. "Alas, my son!" she exclaimed. "What have I done?" The Thebans, seeing this, were seized by sadness and horror.

Bacchus, hoc spectans, dixit, "Pentheus, deorum contemptor, poenas dedit." Bacchus volebat omnibus demonstrare potentiam suam et pericula deorum spernendi.

Bacchus, watching this, said, "Pentheus, the scorner of the gods, has paid the price." Bacchus wanted to show everyone his power and the dangers of defying the gods.

Post mortem Penthei, Thebae in luctu erant. "Regem nostrum perdidimus," dicebant. "Deorum iram timere debemus."

After the death of Pentheus, Thebes was in mourning. "We have lost our king," they said. "We must fear the wrath of the gods."

Fabula Penthei est monitio de periculis sacrorum violatorum. Pentheus, sacra spernens, divinam iram provocavit. Bacchus, deus non solum vini sed etiam ultionis, exemplum statuit. Thebani, postea, Bacchi sacra cum magno timore et reverentia celebraverunt.

The story of Pentheus is a warning about the dangers of violating sacred rites. Pentheus, scorning the sacred, provoked divine wrath. Bacchus, the god not only of wine but also of vengeance, set an example. Afterward, the Thebans celebrated the rites of Bacchus with great fear and reverence.

Nemesis, dea ultionis, Thebas spectabat et annuebat. "Deorum voluntas semper respectanda est," Thebani dicebant.

Nemesis, the goddess of retribution, watched Thebes and nodded. "The will of the gods must always be respected," the Thebans said.

Hic finis est fabulae Penthei, regis Thebani, qui in sua superbia et contemptu deorum periit. Etiam hodie, haec historia nos docet de potentia divina et respectu deorum.

This is the end of the story of Pentheus, the king of Thebes, who perished in his pride and contempt for the gods. Even today, this story teaches us about divine power and respect for the gods.

De Filabus Minyae

In Thebis, urbe Graeciae, Minyae tres filiae, Alcithoe, Leuconoe, et Arsippe, in domo sua erant.

In Thebes, a city of Greece, the three daughters of Minyas, Alcithoe, Leuconoe, and Arsippe, were in their home.

Dum alii Bacchi festa celebrabant, illae domi manebant, fabulas narrantes et texentes.

While others were celebrating the festival of Bacchus, they stayed at home, telling stories and weaving.

Alcithoe coepit fabulam narrare: "Pyramus et Thisbe, duo amantes Babyloniae, a muris separati erant."

Alcithoe began to tell a story: "Pyramus and Thisbe, two lovers of Babylon, were separated by walls."

"Amor eorum fortis erat," addidit Alcithoe, *"sed parentes non concordabant."*

"Their love was strong," added Alcithoe, "but their parents did not agree."

"In secreto," inquit Alcithoe, *"placuerunt nocte sub moro arbore convenire."*

"In secret," said Alcithoe, "they planned to meet at night under a mulberry tree."

Nocte illa, Thisbe prima venit. Subito, leo ad fontem sanguinem bibens apparet. Thisbe videt et in speluncam fugit, velamen relinquens.

That night, Thisbe arrived first. Suddenly, a lion appeared drinking blood at the fountain. Thisbe saw it and fled into a cave, leaving her veil behind.

"Pyramus, postea veniens, velamen laceratum videt," narrat Alcithoe. *"Tristissimus, putat Thisben a leone necatam esse."*

"Pyramus, arriving later, saw the torn veil," Alcithoe narrated. "In great sorrow, he thought Thisbe had been killed by the lion."

Pyramus gladio suo se necat. "Thisbe ex spelunca redit, Pyramum mortuum invenit, et similiter facit."

Pyramus killed himself with his sword. "Thisbe returned from the cave, found Pyramus dead, and did the same."

"Amborum sanguine," finit Alcithoe, *"mori arboris rubefacti sunt." Arsippe et Leuconoe, fabula commotae, tacuerunt.*

"With the blood of both," Alcithoe concluded, "the mulberry tree's fruits were turned red." Arsippe and Leuconoe, moved by the story, remained silent.

Tum Arsippe coepit narrare: "Galatea, pulchra nympha, cyclopem Polyphemum semper spernebat."

Then Arsippe began to tell a story: "Galatea, a beautiful nymph, always scorned the cyclops Polyphemus."

"Sed Acin, iuvenem pulchrum, amabat," dicebat Arsippe.

"But she loved Acis, a handsome young man," said Arsippe.

"Polyphemus, zelotypia captus, Acin vidit et in furore eum interfecit." Arsippe pausavit, "Galatea, maesta, Acin corpus in fluvium mutavit."

"Polyphemus, seized by jealousy, saw Acis and, in a rage, killed him." Arsippe paused, "Galatea, in sorrow, transformed Acis's body into a river."

Postea, Leuconoe fabulam Salmacis et Hermaphroditi coepit: "Salmacis, nympha aquarum, vidit Hermaphroditum et statim eum amavit."

Afterwards, Leuconoe began the story of Salmacis and Hermaphroditus: "Salmacis, a water nymph, saw Hermaphroditus and immediately fell in love with him."

"Sed Hermaphroditus eam reiecit," inquit Leuconoe.

"But Hermaphroditus rejected her," said Leuconoe.

"Salmacis, non decedens, deos oravit ut semper cum Hermaphrodito esset."

"Salmacis, not giving up, prayed to the gods to always be with Hermaphroditus."

"Et ita," finivit Leuconoe, "eorum corpora in unum coniuncta sunt."

"And thus," Leuconoe concluded, "their bodies were joined into one."

Haec fabulae de amore, passione, et mutatione erant.

These stories were about love, passion, and transformation.

Sed Bacchi festa spernentes, filiae Minyae suam metamorphosim nondum sciebant.

But, rejecting the festival of Bacchus, the daughters of Minyas did not yet know of their own transformation.

De Venatione Calydonia

Oeneus, Calydonis rex, sacrificium annuum faciebat.

Oeneus, the king of Calydon, was making an annual sacrifice.

Omnes deos laudabat, sed unam deam neglexit. Diana, dea venationis, irata erat quia non honorata est. "Diana," inquit Oeneus, "non opus est."

He praised all the gods, but he neglected one goddess. Diana, the goddess of the hunt, was angry because she was not honored. "Diana," said Oeneus, "is not needed."

Sed Diana, irata, monstrum terribile misit. Aper ingens, ferus et iracundus, in agros Calydoniae venit.

But Diana, in her anger, sent a terrible monster. A huge, wild, and furious boar came into the fields of Calydon.

Aper terram vastabat, arbores destruebat, homines et animalia necabat. Homines Calydoniae timebant et auxilium petebant. "Quid faciemus?" clamabant.

The boar ravaged the land, destroyed trees, and killed people and animals. The people of Calydon were afraid and begged for help. "What shall we do?" they cried.

Meleager, Oenei filius, audax et fortis, dicebat, "Ego aprum capiam." Convocavit venatores fortissimos, inter quos erat Atalanta, mulier audax et venatrix perita.

Meleager, Oeneus's son, brave and strong, said, "I will catch the boar." He called together the strongest hunters, among whom was Atalanta, a bold woman and skilled huntress.

Venatores, Meleagro duce, in silvas proficiscuntur. In silva densa, vestigia aprum sequuntur. Atalanta, oculis acutis, primum aprum vidit.

The hunters, led by Meleager, set out into the forests. In the thick woods, they followed the boar's tracks. Atalanta, with her sharp eyes, was the first to spot the boar.

Cum sagitta valida, Atalanta aprum vulneravit, sed non interfecit. "Bene fecisti," inquit Meleager, Atalantam admirans. Meleager, cum venatoribus, aprum fortiter pugnavit.

With a strong arrow, Atalanta wounded the boar, but did not kill it. "You have done well," said Meleager, admiring Atalanta. Meleager, with the hunters, fought the boar fiercely.

Dura pugna erat, sed tandem Meleager, cum auxilio Atalantae, aprum interfecit. Calydonii laeti erant et Meleager, victor, caput et pellem aprum Atalantae dedit.

It was a hard fight, but finally Meleager, with Atalanta's help, killed the boar. The people of Calydon were joyful, and Meleager, victorious, gave the boar's head and hide to Atalanta.

Althaea, Meleagri mater, hoc audiebat et irata erat. "Meleager, filius meus, quid fecisti?" exclamavit. Meleager responsum non dedit, sed mater furens erat.

Althaea, Meleager's mother, heard this and was angry. "Meleager, my son, what have you done?" she exclaimed. Meleager did not answer, but his mother was furious.

Althaea lignum, fato Meleagri connectum, comburebat. Meleager, subito, dolorem magnum sentiebat. "Mater, cur?" clamavit, sed sero erat.

Althaea burned the log that was connected to Meleager's fate. Meleager suddenly felt great pain. "Mother, why?" he cried, but it was too late.

Meleager, consumptus dolore, in avem mutatus est. Althaea, facti sui paenitens, se ipsam interfecit. "Heu, me miseram!" inquit, et mortua est.

Meleager, consumed by pain, was transformed into a bird. Althaea, regretting her actions, killed herself. "Alas, wretched me!" she said, and she died.

Fabula de Calydonio apre non solum de audacia, sed etiam de ira et fato narrat. Meleager et Atalanta exempla sunt virtutis, sed Althaea irae pericula monstrat.

The story of the Calydonian boar tells not only of courage but also of anger and fate. Meleager and Atalanta are examples of virtue, but Althaea shows the dangers of rage.

De Perseo et Andromeda

In Graecia antiqua, Perseus, Acrisii nepos, ad insulam Seriphum navigavit.

In ancient Greece, Perseus, the grandson of Acrisius, sailed to the island of Seriphos.

Polydectes, rex insulae, Perseum ad difficillimum opus misit: caput Gorgonis Medusae adferre.

Polydectes, the king of the island, sent Perseus on a very difficult task: to bring back the head of the Gorgon Medusa.

Perseus, vir audax, consensit et ad Graeas, Medusae sorores, ivit. "Auxilium vestrum peto," Perseus dixit. Graeae, cum reluctarentur, tandem consenserunt.

Perseus, a bold man, agreed and went to the Graeae, the sisters of Medusa. "I seek your help," Perseus said. The Graeae, though reluctant, eventually agreed.

Dei, Persei audaciam admirantes, arma ei dederunt: galeam, quae eum invisibilem faciebat, talaria, alata calceamenta, et scutum fulgens. "His armis, Medusam vincere potes," dixerunt.

The gods, admiring Perseus' bravery, gave him weapons: a helmet that made him invisible, winged sandals, and a shining shield. "With these weapons, you can defeat Medusa," they said.

Perseus, armis instructus, ad Medusam ivit. Eam dormientem invenit et, speculo in scuto utendo, eius caput sine periculo amputavit. Ex Medusae sanguine Pegasus, equus alatus, natus est.

Armed with these, Perseus went to Medusa. He found her sleeping and, using the reflection in the shield, safely cut off her head. From Medusa's blood, Pegasus, the winged horse, was born.

Perseus, iter faciens, ad Andromedam venit. Eam vidit ad saxum alligatam, monstro marino immolandam. "Cur hic es?" Perseus rogavit. Andromeda, lacrimans, historiam suam narravit.

As Perseus journeyed, he came upon Andromeda. He saw her tied to a rock, about to be sacrificed to a sea monster. "Why are you here?" Perseus asked. Andromeda, crying, told her story.

Perseus Andromedae parentes convenit. "Filiam vestram servabo," promisit. Monstrum mare, horrendum et ingens, apparuit. Perseus, armatus et paratus, ad pugnam processit.

Perseus met Andromeda's parents. "I will save your daughter," he promised. The sea monster, terrifying and enormous, appeared. Perseus, armed and ready, stepped forward to fight.

Perseus, cum audacia et arte, monstrum interfecit. Andromeda liberata est, et omnes gratias ei egerunt. Perseus, Andromedam amans, eam uxorem ducere voluit.

With courage and skill, Perseus killed the monster. Andromeda was freed, and everyone thanked him. Perseus, loving Andromeda, wished to marry her.

Nuptiae inter Perseum et Andromedam celebratae sunt. Sed Phineus, Andromedae patruus, iratus venit. "Andromeda mea est!" clamavit Phineus, gladium stringens.

The marriage between Perseus and Andromeda was celebrated. But Phineus, Andromeda's uncle, came angrily. "Andromeda is mine!" shouted Phineus, drawing his sword.

Phineus et sui milites Perseum oppugnaverunt. Sed Perseus, ultimum auxilium habens, caput Medusae ostendit. Phineus et comites eius in lapides statim mutati sunt.

Phineus and his soldiers attacked Perseus. But Perseus, having a final trick, showed Medusa's head. Phineus and his companions were instantly turned to stone.

Perseus et Andromeda, post haec pericula, una feliciter vixerunt. Perseus, vir fortis et iustus, laudem et gloriam in toto regno habuit. Andromeda, uxor eius, exemplum virtutis et pulchritudinis erat.

Perseus and Andromeda, after these dangers, lived happily together. Perseus, a strong and just man, earned praise and glory throughout the kingdom. Andromeda, his wife, was an example of virtue and beauty.

Fabula de Perseo et Andromeda non solum de audacia et amore narrat, sed etiam de fatis et deorum voluntate. Eorum historia in arte et litteris per saecula mansit, exemplar heroismi et amoris veri.

The story of Perseus and Andromeda is not only about courage and love, but also about fate and the will of the gods. Their tale has endured for centuries in art and literature, as an example of heroism and true love.

De Pyramo et Thisbe

In antiqua Babylone, Pyramus et Thisbe, duo iuvenes, vicini vivebant.

In ancient Babylon, Pyramus and Thisbe, two young people, lived as neighbors.

Ardentissime se amabant, sed eorum parentes matrimonia inter eos prohibebant. "Non potestis esse una," parentes dicebant.

They loved each other passionately, but their parents forbade marriage between them. "You cannot be together," their parents said.

Tamen, Pyramus et Thisbe, amore invicti, secreto communicabant. Parvam rimam in muro, qui domos eorum separabat, invenerunt. Per hanc rimam, voces amoris susurrabant.

However, Pyramus and Thisbe, undefeated by love, communicated in secret. They found a small crack in the wall that separated their houses. Through this crack, they whispered words of love.

"In secreto nocte conveniemus," Pyramus susurravit. "Sub arbore moro," respondit Thisbe. Cor eorum plenum spe et amore erat.

"We will meet in secret at night," Pyramus whispered. "Under the mulberry tree," Thisbe replied. Their hearts were full of hope and love.

Nocte constituta, Thisbe prima ad locum convenit. Sub moro sedens, subito leonem vidit. Territa, fugit et velamen reliquit. Leo, sanguinem bibens, velamen laceravit.

On the appointed night, Thisbe arrived at the place first. Sitting under the mulberry tree, she suddenly saw a lion. Terrified, she fled and left her veil behind. The lion, drinking blood, tore the veil.

Pyramus, paulo post, advenit et vidit velamen laceratum. "O deorum crudelitas!" exclamavit. Credens Thisben a leone necatam, gladio suo se necavit.

Pyramus arrived shortly after and saw the torn veil. "Oh, the cruelty of the gods!" he exclaimed. Believing Thisbe had been killed by the lion, he killed himself with his sword.

Thisbe, rediens, Pyramum iacentem invenit. "Pyrame!" clamavit. "Quid fecisti?" Intellexit quid accidisset et mortem suam elegit. "Ero tecum in morte," dixit et se necavit.

Thisbe, returning, found Pyramus lying dead. "Pyramus!" she cried. "What have you done?" Realizing what had happened, she chose to die as well. "I will be with you in death," she said and killed herself.

Eorum sanguine, mori arboris bacas rubras fecit. Arbor, antea alba, nunc rubra erat, amoris et mortis symbolum.

Their blood stained the berries of the mulberry tree red. The tree, once white, was now red, a symbol of love and death.

Parentes, mortibus natorum docti, moestitiam et paenitentiam gerebant. "Amor eorum purus erat," dicebant. "Nos erravimus."

The parents, taught by the deaths of their children, mourned and felt regret. "Their love was pure," they said. "We were wrong."

Pyrami et Thisbes amor, in morte perfectus, per saecula celebratus est. Fabula eorum, tristis sed pulchra, amoris potestatem demonstrat.

The love of Pyramus and Thisbe, made perfect in death, has been celebrated for centuries. Their story, sad but beautiful, demonstrates the power of love.

Pyramus et Thisbe, in fabula Ovidii, exemplum amoris veri et tragici sunt. Eorum historia, de passionibus et sacrificiis narrans, adhuc corda tangit.

Pyramus and Thisbe, in Ovid's tale, are an example of true and tragic love. Their story, telling of passions and sacrifices, still touches hearts.

Ovidius, in "Metamorphoses", hanc fabulam antiquam renovavit. Per eam, themata amoris et mortis exploravit, quae in arte et litteris per aetates repetita sunt.

Ovid, in his "Metamorphoses", revived this ancient story. Through it, he explored the themes of love and death, which have been repeated in art and literature throughout the ages.

De Leucothoe et Clytie

In antiqua Babylone, Leucothoe, virgo pulchra et casta, a Sole, deo splendido, amabatur.

In ancient Babylon, Leucothoe, a beautiful and chaste maiden, was loved by the Sun, the radiant god.

Sol, per caelum volans, Leucothoen vidit et statim amore captus est.

The Sun, flying across the sky, saw Leucothoe and was immediately captivated by love.

Clytie, nympha alia, Solem etiam amabat. Sed cum vidit Solem Leucothoen amare, invidia mota est. "Cur Leucothoe?" se interrogavit. "Cur non ego?"

Clytie, another nymph, also loved the Sun. But when she saw that the Sun loved Leucothoe, she was moved by jealousy. "Why Leucothoe?" she asked herself. "Why not me?"

Clytie, amore et invidia plena, consilium cepit. Ad Solem ivit et dixit, "Sol, scisne quis te amat? Leucothoe, virgo Babylonis." Sol, audito hoc, iratus et confusus erat.

Clytie, full of love and jealousy, made a plan. She went to the Sun and said, "Sun, do you know who loves you? Leucothoe, the maiden of Babylon." Upon hearing this, the Sun was angry and confused.

Sol, ira ductus, terram movit et Leucothoen vivam defodit. Sub terra, Leucothoe a radiis Solis mutata est. In arborem thuris, fragrantem et pulchram, conversa est.

The Sun, driven by anger, moved the earth and buried Leucothoe alive. Beneath the ground, Leucothoe was transformed by the rays of the Sun. She became a fragrant and beautiful frankincense tree.

Clytie, videns quod fecerat, paenitentia et amore captata, Solem numquam deseruit. Dies et noctes, sine cibo et aqua, Solem spectabat. Sed Sol eam numquam respexit.

Clytie, seeing what she had done, overwhelmed by regret and love, never left the Sun. Day and night, without food or water, she gazed at the Sun. But the Sun never looked back at her.

Novem dies transierunt, Clytie adhuc Solem spectans. Tandem, in terram radices misit et in florem mutata est. Heliotropium facta est, flos qui semper solem sequitur.

Nine days passed, and Clytie continued to watch the Sun. Finally, she sent roots into the ground and was transformed into a flower. She became a heliotrope, a flower that always follows the Sun.

Fabula de Leucothoe et Clytie docet de amore non redito et periculis invidiae.

The story of Leucothoe and Clytie teaches about unreturned love and the dangers of jealousy.

Demonstrat etiam potestatem et inconstantiam Solis, et quomodo amor inter deos et mortales movet.

It also shows the power and inconstancy of the Sun, and how love between gods and mortals stirs emotions.

Metamorphosis Clyties ostendit naturam eius desiderii et tristitiam amoris non correspondi. Heliotropium facta, Clytie symbolum est amoris desperati et spei inanis.

Clytie's transformation reveals the nature of her desire and the sadness of unreciprocated love. Becoming a heliotrope, Clytie is a symbol of desperate love and futile hope.

Ovidius, in hac fabula, lectoribus mirabilia naturae et mutationes cordis humani monstrat. "Amor," inquit, "potest et pulcher et periculosus esse."

Ovid, in this story, shows readers the wonders of nature and the transformations of the human heart. "Love," he says, "can be both beautiful and dangerous."

Fabula finit, sed manet exemplum Clyties et Leucothoes, duarum feminarum a amore et deorum voluntate affectarum. Eorum historia nos docet de potentia amoris et doloribus, quos saepe fert.

The story ends, but the example of Clytie and Leucothoe remains, two women affected by love and the will of the gods. Their story teaches us about the power of love and the pains it often brings.

De Raptu Proserpinae

In Sicilia, insula pulchra, Proserpina, Cereris filia, flores colligebat.

In Sicily, a beautiful island, Proserpina, the daughter of Ceres, was gathering flowers.

Erat virgo pulchra et innocens, gaudens in naturae pulchritudine.

She was a beautiful and innocent maiden, delighting in the beauty of nature.

Pluto, inferorum rex, terram invisit et Proserpinam vidit. "Ea erit mea," inquit Pluto, amore et desiderio captus. Proserpinam rapuit et ad inferos duxit.

Pluto, the king of the underworld, visited the earth and saw Proserpina. "She will be mine," said Pluto, seized by love and desire. He abducted Proserpina and took her to the underworld.

Ceres, dea frugum et maternitatis, filiam suam ubique quaerebat. "Ubi est Proserpina mea?" clamabat. Sed nemo respondere poterat; Proserpina ablata erat.

Ceres, the goddess of crops and motherhood, searched everywhere for her daughter. "Where is my Proserpina?" she cried. But no one could answer; Proserpina had been taken.

Sol, qui omnia videt, Cereri veritatem narravit. "Pluto, frater tuus, Proserpinam rapuit," dixit Sol. Ceres, hoc audito, irata et maesta facta est.

The Sun, who sees everything, told Ceres the truth. "Pluto, your brother, has abducted Proserpina," said the Sun. Hearing this, Ceres became angry and sorrowful.

Ceres, dolore affecta, terram sterilem fecit. Fruges non creverunt, flores non aperuerunt. "Dum filia mea abest, terra non fructificabit," inquit Ceres.

Ceres, stricken with grief, made the earth barren. Crops did not grow, and flowers did not bloom. "While my daughter is gone, the earth will not bear fruit," said Ceres.

Iuppiter, deorum rex et frater Cereris, intervenit. "Non potest terra sterili manere," dixit Iuppiter. "Pacem inter vos faciamus."

Jupiter, the king of the gods and Ceres' brother, intervened. "The earth cannot remain barren," said Jupiter. "Let us make peace between you."

Decretum est ut Proserpina partem anni cum matre in terra, partem anni cum Plutone in inferis ageret. Sic factum est, et Proserpina regina inferorum et terrae facta est.

It was decreed that Proserpina would spend part of the year with her mother on earth, and part of the year with Pluto in the underworld. And so it happened, and Proserpina became the queen of both the underworld and the earth.

Cum Proserpina in terra est, Ceres laeta est et terra fructum fert. Cum in inferis est, Ceres maestitiam habet et terra sterilis fit. Sic origines temporum anni et frugum explicatae sunt.

When Proserpina is on earth, Ceres is joyful, and the earth bears fruit. When she is in the underworld, Ceres is sorrowful, and the earth becomes barren. Thus, the origins of the seasons and the growth of crops are explained.

Fabula non solum de temporibus anni, sed etiam de amoris materni potestate et dolore separationis narrat. Proserpinae rapina symbolum est transitionis a iuventute ad maturitatem.

The story is not only about the seasons but also about the power of maternal love and the pain of separation. Proserpina's abduction is a symbol of the transition from youth to maturity.

Cereris luctus et ira demonstrant quomodo natura humanae passioni respondet. Ovidius hoc mytho utitur ad explicandas mutationes naturae per annos.

Ceres' grief and anger show how nature responds to human passion. Ovid uses this myth to explain the changes in nature throughout the years.

Fabula Proserpinae in arte et litteris per saecula repraesentata est, exemplum amoris, doloris, et potentiae deorum. Proserpina et Ceres nobis ostendunt quam profunde amor matris et filiae sit.

The story of Proserpina has been represented in art and literature for centuries as an example of love, sorrow, and the power of the gods. Proserpina and Ceres show us how deep the love between mother and daughter is.

In hac fabula, Ovidius lectoribus potentiam deorum et fati monstrat, simulque naturam humanam et divinam explorat. Proserpinae rapina in memoria manet, fabula aeterna de amore, potestate, et mutatione vitae.

In this story, Ovid shows readers the power of the gods and fate while also exploring both human and divine nature. Proserpina's abduction remains in memory as an eternal tale of love, power, and the transformation of life.

Perseus et Phineus

In antiquis diebus, Perseus, filius magni Iovis, ad regis Cephei convivium invitatus est.

In ancient days, Perseus, the son of great Jupiter, was invited to the feast of King Cepheus.

Perseus, vir fortis et audax, multa proelia vicerat et multas terras visitaverat. Cum ad regiam Cephei venit, omnes eum mirabantur propter eius fortitudinem et historias de proeliis suis.

Perseus, a strong and bold man, had won many battles and visited many lands. When he came to the palace of Cepheus, everyone admired him for his bravery and the stories of his battles.

Inter convivas erat Phineus, frater regis Cephei. Phineus, vir ambitiosus et invidus, Perseum non amabat. Tamen, more hospitii,

Phineus Perseum ad convivium invitavit. "Salve, Persee," dixit Phineus. "Fama tua nos omnes antecedit. Dic nobis de tuis mirabilibus factis."

Among the guests was Phineus, the brother of King Cepheus. Phineus, an ambitious and jealous man, did not like Perseus. However, following the custom of hospitality, Phineus invited Perseus to the feast. "Greetings, Perseus," said Phineus. "Your fame precedes you. Tell us of your wondrous deeds."

Perseus, accepto honore, coepit narrare. "Gratias tibi ago, Phinee," respondit Perseus. "In unum ex meis proeliis, contra terribilem monstrum maris, Medusam, pugnavi."

Perseus, receiving the honor, began to speak. "Thank you, Phineus," responded Perseus. "In one of my battles, I fought against the terrible sea monster, Medusa."

Tunc Perseus caput Medusae, quod adhuc terribile et potentissimum erat, ostendit. Omnes convivae territi erant. Caput Medusae magicum erat, et omnes qui in illud aspiciebant in saxum mutabantur.

Then Perseus revealed the head of Medusa, which was still terrifying and extremely powerful. All the guests were frightened. The head of Medusa was magical, and anyone who looked at it was turned into stone.

Statim, omnes convivae, excepto Perseo, in saxa conversi sunt. Phineus, videns hoc, magno timore affectus est. Phineus, tremens, ad Perseum accessit et pacem petivit. "Persee, quaeso, ignosce mihi," rogavit Phineus. "Non volui tibi malum. Parce mihi!"

Immediately, all the guests, except for Perseus, were turned into stone. Phineus, seeing this, was struck with great fear. Trembling, Phineus approached Perseus and begged for peace. "Perseus, please, forgive me," Phineus begged. "I did not mean you any harm. Spare me!"

Perseus, corde generoso, Phineo ignovit. "Phinee, te ignosco," dixit Perseus. "Tu et tui amici in saxa non manebitis."

Perseus, with a generous heart, forgave Phineus. "Phineus, I forgive you," said Perseus. "You and your friends will not remain as stones."

Et magica vi sua, Perseus omnes convivas ad pristinam formam restituit.

And with his magical power, Perseus restored all the guests to their original form.

Posteae, Perseus de aliis suis proeliis narravit. Deinde, de aventura sua in Aethiopia locutus est. "In Aethiopia, monstrum marinum terram vastabat," incepit Perseus. "Monstrum illud Andromedam, filiam Cephei, devorare volebat."

Afterward, Perseus told of his other battles. Then, he spoke about his adventure in Ethiopia. "In Ethiopia, a sea monster was ravaging the land," began Perseus. "That monster wanted to devour Andromeda, the daughter of Cepheus."

Perseus, Andromedam videns, statim eam amavit. "Monstro marino pugnavi," continuavit Perseus. "Et, Deorum auxilio, monstrum vici."

Perseus, upon seeing Andromeda, immediately fell in love with her. "I fought the sea monster," Perseus continued, "and, with the help of the gods, I defeated it."

Andromeda, liberata, Perseo gratias egit. Cepheus, Andromedae pater, Perseo filiam suam in matrimonium dedit.

Andromeda, freed, thanked Perseus. Cepheus, Andromeda's father, gave his daughter in marriage to Perseus.

Tandem, Perseus et Andromeda magnas nuptias celebraverunt. Sed in medio festo, Phineus et sui homines Perseum oppugnare conati sunt. Phineus, iratus quod Andromeda Perseo data erat, gladium sumpserat et ad Perseum cucurrit.

Finally, Perseus and Andromeda celebrated a grand wedding. But in the middle of the celebration, Phineus and his men tried to attack Perseus. Phineus, angry that Andromeda had been given to Perseus, took up his sword and ran toward Perseus.

Sed Perseus, non timens, caput Medusae ostendit. Phineus et sui homines in saxa mutati sunt. Perseus, victor, cum Andromeda in pace vixit, et Phineus cum suis in saxo mansit, sempiternum monumentum irae et invidiae.

But Perseus, without fear, showed the head of Medusa. Phineus and his men were turned into stone. Perseus, victorious, lived in peace with Andromeda, while Phineus and his men remained as stone, an eternal monument to anger and jealousy.

Pallas et Musae

In antiquo monte Helicone, Musae, deae artium et carminum, habitabant.

In ancient Mount Helicon, the Muses, goddesses of the arts and songs, lived.

Illae sorores novem erant, pulchrae et sapientiae plenae. Unum diem, Pallas Athena, dea sapientiae, ad montem Helicone venit ut Musas visitaret.

They were nine sisters, beautiful and full of wisdom. One day, Pallas Athena, the goddess of wisdom, came to Mount Helicon to visit the Muses.

Pallas Athena, cum ad montem venit, Musas invenit cantantes. "Salvete, Musae," dixit Pallas. "Quid cantatis?"

When Pallas Athena arrived at the mountain, she found the Muses singing. "Greetings, Muses," said Pallas. "What are you singing?"

Musae responderunt, "Cantamus de gigantum bello contra deos. Est fabula magna et antiqua."

The Muses replied, "We are singing about the war of the giants against the gods. It is a great and ancient story."

Dum Musae cantabant, Pegasus, equus alatus mirabilis, super montem volabat. Pegasus, pede suo, fontem Hippocrenen aperuit. Aqua fontis erat clara et pura, et omnes mirabantur.

While the Muses were singing, Pegasus, the marvelous winged horse, flew over the mountain. With his hoof, Pegasus opened the Hippocrene spring. The water of the spring was clear and pure, and all marveled.

Interim, Pyreneus, rex Thraciae, ad montem venit. Pyreneus Musas decipere voluit. "Musae," inquit, "venite ad meam regiam. Ibi tutae eritis."

Meanwhile, Pyreneus, the king of Thrace, came to the mountain. Pyreneus wanted to deceive the Muses. "Muses," he said, "come to my palace. There you will be safe."

Sed Musae Pyreneum non credebant. Tunc, magica arte, in aves se mutaverunt et volaverunt ut Pyreneum fugerent. Pyreneus, iratus et deceptus, se ex alto monte praecipitavit.

But the Muses did not believe Pyreneus. Then, by magical art, they transformed into birds and flew away to escape him. Pyreneus, angry and deceived, threw himself from the high mountain.

Postea, Musae aliam fabulam narraverunt. "Narrabimus de Tyrrheno pirata et Galatea," dixit una Musa. "Piratae Tyrrheni, Galateam nympham amantes, in delphinos mutati sunt."

Afterward, the Muses told another story. "We will tell of the Tyrrhenian pirate and Galatea," said one Muse. "The Tyrrhenian pirates, who loved the nymph Galatea, were turned into dolphins."

Then, the Muses sang about Ceres, the goddess of crops, and her daughter Proserpina. "Proserpina was abducted by Pluto, god of the underworld," another Muse explained.

Cerere, filiam suam quaerens, per totum mundum vagabatur. Ad Cyaneam fontem venit, ubi Cyane, nympha, Cereri veritatem de raptu narravit.

Ceres, searching for her daughter, wandered through the entire world. She came to the Cyanean spring, where Cyane, a nymph, told Ceres the truth about the abduction.

Cerere, irata et tristis, terram sterilitate afflixit. Homines fame laborabant et Cererem orabant. "Cerere, dea magna," clamabant, "terram benedic!"

Ceres, angry and sad, afflicted the earth with barrenness. People suffered from hunger and prayed to Ceres. "Ceres, great goddess," they cried, "bless the land!"

Tandem, Cerere filiam suam recuperavit, sed conventione inter deos, Proserpina partem anni in inferis manebat et partem in terra cum matre.

At last, Ceres regained her daughter, but by an agreement among the gods, Proserpina would spend part of the year in the underworld and part of the year on earth with her mother.

Musae finem fabulae cantaverunt. Pallas Athena, audiens haec, Musis gratias egit. "Fabulae vestrae non solum pulchrae sunt, sed etiam doctae," inquit Pallas. "Gratias vobis ago pro sapientia vestra."

The Muses finished their tale. Pallas Athena, hearing this, thanked the Muses. "Your stories are not only beautiful but also wise," said Pallas. "Thank you for your wisdom."

Musae, laetae ob verba Palladis, ad cantum redierunt. Pallas Athena ex monte discessit, Musas in arte sua relinquens.

The Muses, happy with Pallas's words, returned to their song. Pallas Athena left the mountain, leaving the Muses to their craft.

Monte Helicone relicto, Pallas Athena coelum petivit, Musarum cantus in mente servans, et deorum consilium de terrae frugum statu cogitavit.

After leaving Mount Helicon, Pallas Athena ascended to the heavens, keeping the Muses' song in her mind and pondering the gods' counsel about the state of the earth's crops.

Arethusa et Alpheus

In antiqua Graecia, in insula Sicilia, fabula de Arethusa, nympha, et Alpheo, fluvio, narratur.

In ancient Greece, on the island of Sicily, the story of Arethusa, a nymph, and Alpheus, a river, is told.

Arethusa, nympha pulcherrima et a Diana, dea venationis, dilecta, in silvis et pratis vagabatur.

Arethusa, a very beautiful nymph and beloved by Diana, goddess of the hunt, wandered in the forests and meadows.

Unum diem, Alpheus, fluvius magnus, Arethusam vidit et statim amore in eam incensus est. "O Arethusa," inquit Alpheus, "es pulcherrima omnium nympharum. Te amo et tecum esse volo."

One day, Alpheus, a great river, saw Arethusa and immediately fell in love with her. "Oh Arethusa," said Alpheus, "you are the most beautiful of all the nymphs. I love you and want to be with you."

Arethusa, territa et Alphei amorem nolens, fugere coepit. Per silvas et montes cucurrit, sed Alpheus eam semper sequebatur. Tandem, Arethusa, fessa et desperata, Dianam oravit. "Diana, dea venationis," clamavit, "adiuva me! Alpheus me persequitur et ego eum non amo!"

Arethusa, frightened and rejecting Alpheus's love, began to flee. She ran through forests and mountains, but Alpheus always followed her. Finally, exhausted and desperate, Arethusa prayed to Diana. "Diana, goddess of the hunt," she cried, "help me! Alpheus is chasing me, and I do not love him!"

Diana, audiens preces Arethusae, eam in fontem mutavit. Corpus Arethusae in aquam conversum est, et sic Alpheo effugere potuit.

Diana, hearing Arethusa's prayers, transformed her into a spring. Arethusa's body turned into water, and thus she was able to escape Alpheus.

Sed Alpheus, amore ardens, suum cursum mutavit et ad Siciliam, ubi Arethusa erat, fluebat.

But Alpheus, burning with love, changed his course and flowed to Sicily, where Arethusa was.

In Sicilia, Alpheus, ut fluvius, Arethusam, nunc fontem, invenit. Arethusa, fontem formans, adhuc Alpheum timebat.

In Sicily, Alpheus, as a river, found Arethusa, now a spring. Arethusa, now in the form of a spring, still feared Alpheus.

Sed Alpheus, in aquas suas, cum Arethusa iunctus est. Sic, in aquis dulcibus Siciliae, Arethusa et Alpheus semper simul erant.

But Alpheus joined his waters with Arethusa's. Thus, in the fresh waters of Sicily, Arethusa and Alpheus were always together.

Dum haec fiebant, Arethusa Cereri, dea frugum, occurrit. "Cerere," inquit Arethusa, "Proserpina, filia tua, a Pluto raptata est. Scio ubi est."

While this was happening, Arethusa met Ceres, the goddess of crops. "Ceres," said Arethusa, "Proserpina, your daughter, was kidnapped by Pluto. I know where she is."

Cerere, de terra sterili sollicita, auxilium Arethusae quaesivit. "Arethusa," rogavit Cerere, "potestne aqua tua terram fecundam facere?"

Ceres, concerned about the barren earth, sought Arethusa's help. "Arethusa," asked Ceres, "can your water make the land fertile?"

Arethusa respondit, "Ita, Cerere. Aqua mea frugibus fertilitatem dabit." Et aqua Arethusae per Siciliam fluebat, terram fecundans. Terra iterum frugibus abundabat, et homines laeti erant.

Arethusa replied, "Yes, Ceres. My water will give fertility to the crops." And Arethusa's water flowed through Sicily, making the land fertile. The land once again became abundant with crops, and the people were joyful.

Homines, frugum copia gaudentes, Cereri festa magna celebraverunt. "Gratias tibi, Cerere," clamabant, "pro frugibus et fertilitate."

The people, rejoicing in the abundance of crops, celebrated great festivals for Ceres. "Thank you, Ceres," they shouted, "for the crops and fertility."

Cerere, videns terram frugibus plenam, laeta erat. Grata Arethusae auxilio, terram benedixit. "Arethusa," dixit Cerere, "gratias tibi ago. Propter te, terra nostra iterum frugibus abundat."

Ceres, seeing the land full of crops, was happy. Grateful for Arethusa's help, she blessed the land. "Arethusa," said Ceres, "thank you. Because of you, our land is abundant with crops once again."

In templo, Cerere et Proserpina, eius filia, magnis honoribus fruebantur. Omnes deorum in Cererem et Proserpinam gratiam agebant, quia terram fecundaverunt.

In the temple, Ceres and her daughter Proserpina were greatly honored. Everyone gave thanks to Ceres and Proserpina, for they had made the land fertile.

Sic finitur fabula de Arethusa et Alpheo, de amoris potestate et terrae fertilitate. Haec fabula antiqua adhuc in Sicilia narratur, et Arethusa et Alpheus in aquis dulcibus insulae manent, amoris et fertilitatis symbolum.

Thus ends the tale of Arethusa and Alpheus, about the power of love and the fertility of the land. This ancient story is still told in Sicily, and Arethusa and Alpheus remain in the fresh waters of the island, a symbol of love and fertility.

Triptolemus

In antiquis temporibus, Ceres, dea frugum et agriculturae, Triptolemo, iuveni Graeco, munus mirabile dedit.

In ancient times, Ceres, goddess of crops and agriculture, gave a marvelous gift to Triptolemus, a young Greek.

Munus erat currus volans, trahitur a serpentibus. Triptolemus, currum accipiens, miratus est.

The gift was a flying chariot, drawn by serpents. Triptolemus, upon receiving the chariot, was amazed.

Ceres Triptolemo dixit, "Triptoleme, tibi currum volantem do. Cum hoc curru, per orbem terrarum volabis frumentum spargens. Sic homines artem agriculturae discere possunt."

Ceres said to Triptolemus, "Triptolemus, I give you this flying chariot. With this chariot, you will fly across the world, scattering grain. In this way, people can learn the art of agriculture."

Triptolemus, gratias agens, in currum ascendit et coepit per orbem volare. Ubi terram invenit, frumentum spargebat. Primum, terra arida et sterilis erat, sed postquam Triptolemus frumentum sparsit, frumentum coepit crescere.

Triptolemus, giving thanks, ascended the chariot and began flying across the world. Wherever he found land, he scattered grain. At first, the land was dry and barren, but after Triptolemus spread the grain, crops began to grow.

Agricolae, frumentum videntes, laeti erant. "Ecce," inquit unus, "frumentum in terra nostra crescit! Numquam ante vidimus talia. Dea Ceres nos benedixit!"

The farmers, seeing the grain, were joyful. "Look," said one, "grain is growing on our land! We have never seen anything like this before. The goddess Ceres has blessed us!"

Triptolemus per multas terras volavit, agricolis artem agriculturae docens. Homines per orbem frumento gaudebant et Cererem laudabant.

Triptolemus flew over many lands, teaching farmers the art of agriculture. People around the world rejoiced in the grain and praised Ceres.

Post multos dies, Triptolemus ad Scythiam, terram longinquam et barbaricam, venit. Lyncus, rex Scythiae, eum vidit et invidia motus est. "Quis est hic qui per caelum volat?" interrogavit Lyncus.

After many days, Triptolemus arrived in Scythia, a distant and barbaric land. Lyncus, the king of Scythia, saw him and was moved by envy. "Who is this that flies through the sky?" Lyncus asked.

Consilium cepit Lyncus Triptolemum interficere, ut currum eius sibi caperet. Nocte, cum Triptolemus dormiebat, Lyncus ad eum cum gladio accessit.

Lyncus planned to kill Triptolemus to take his chariot for himself. At night, while Triptolemus slept, Lyncus approached him with a sword.

Sed Ceres, quae omnia videt, Lyncum in lyncem mutavit. Lyncus, fera silvestris factus, in silvas fugit. Triptolemus, incolumis, expergefactus est et quid accidisset miratus est.

But Ceres, who sees all, transformed Lyncus into a lynx. Lyncus, now a wild beast, fled into the forests. Triptolemus, unharmed, awoke and wondered what had happened.

Cum ad Graeciam rediit, Triptolemus Cereri narravit quae in Scythia acciderant. Ceres, audito Lynci conatu, Triptolemo gratias egit. "Triptoleme," inquit, "tu fidus et fortis es. Agricolae artes per orbem diffudisti."

When he returned to Greece, Triptolemus told Ceres what had happened in Scythia. Ceres, hearing of Lyncus's attempt, thanked Triptolemus. "Triptolemus," she said, "you are loyal and brave. You have spread the art of agriculture across the world."

Homines, ubique in terra, frumento et Cereri benedicebant. Ceres et Triptolemus in templo honorabantur. Terra, propter Triptolemi laborem, frugum copia referta est.

People everywhere on earth blessed Ceres and Triptolemus for the grain. Ceres and Triptolemus were honored in the temple. Because of Triptolemus's work, the earth was filled with an abundance of crops.

Sic finitur fabula Triptolemi, qui cum curru volante per orbem volavit et hominibus artem agriculturae docuit. Hoc modo, Ceres, dea frugum, terram et homines benedixit, et Triptolemus semper in memoria hominum manet, heros agriculturae et dator vitae.

Thus ends the story of Triptolemus, who flew across the world in a flying chariot and taught people the art of agriculture. In this way, Ceres, the goddess of crops, blessed the earth and humanity, and Triptolemus remains forever in the memory of people, a hero of agriculture and giver of life.

Orpheus et Eurydice

In antiquis Graeciae temporibus, Orpheus, praeclarus cantor et lyrae magister, vivebat.

In ancient times in Greece, Orpheus, a famous singer and master of the lyre, lived.

Uxorem habebat nomine Eurydicen, femina pulcherrima et amata. Orpheus et Eurydice magnopere se amabant, et eorum amor omnibus notus erat.

He had a wife named Eurydice, a very beautiful and beloved woman. Orpheus and Eurydice loved each other greatly, and their love was known to all.

Triste fatum evenit. Eurydice, dum in pratis ambulat, a venenato serpente morsa est. Morsa, statim mortua est.

A sad fate occurred. Eurydice, while walking in the meadows, was bitten by a venomous snake. Bitten, she died immediately.

Orpheus, uxorem suam amisso, maestus et desperatus erat. "Eurydice mea," Orpheus flevit, "non possum sine te vivere!"

Orpheus, having lost his wife, was sad and desperate. "My Eurydice," Orpheus wept, "I cannot live without you!"

Orpheus, amore magno motus, audacem consilium cepit. Decidit ad inferos descendere ut uxorem suam a morte revocaret. Lyram suam tollens, ad inferos descendit, cantans carmina tristia et dulcia.

Orpheus, moved by great love, made a bold decision. He decided to descend to the underworld to bring back his wife from death. Taking up his lyre, he descended to the underworld, singing sad and sweet songs.

In inferis, canticis suis Orpheus omnes movit, etiam deos inferos. Pluto, deus inferorum, et Proserpina, regina inferorum, canticis Orphei commoti sunt. "Nunquam antea talia carmina audivimus," dixerunt. "Tua amor verus et carmina tua nos moverunt."

In the underworld, Orpheus moved everyone with his songs, even the gods of the underworld. Pluto, the god of the underworld, and Proserpina, queen of the underworld, were moved by Orpheus's songs. "We have never heard such songs before," they said. "Your true love and your music have touched us."

Pluto et Proserpina Orpheo dixerunt, "Eurydicen tecum ad superos redire sinemus. Sed una conditio est: dum ascenditis, tu Eurydicen ante non respicias."

Pluto and Proserpina said to Orpheus, "We will allow Eurydice to return with you to the land of the living. But there is one condition: as you ascend, you must not look back at her."

Orpheus, laetus et gratus, conditionem accepit. Coepit cum Eurydice ascendere. Sed, prope ad exitum inferorum, dubitatione captus est. "Eurydice mea, me sequeris?" anxie rogavit.

Orpheus, happy and grateful, accepted the condition. He began to ascend with Eurydice. But, near the exit of the underworld, he was seized with doubt. "My Eurydice, are you following me?" he anxiously asked.

Non respondente Eurydice, Orpheus respexit. Eurydice, adhuc in limine inferorum, iterum ad umbras rediit. Orpheus, errore suo perterritus, Eurydicem amissam flevit.

With Eurydice not responding, Orpheus looked back. Eurydice, still at the threshold of the underworld, was pulled back to the shadows. Orpheus, terrified by his mistake, wept for the loss of Eurydice.

Orpheus, ad superos reversus, maestus et solus erat. Per silvas errabat, cantans carmina tristia. Omnia animalia et arbores carminibus eius movebantur. Nihil eum consolari poterat.

Orpheus, having returned to the land of the living, was sad and alone. He wandered through the forests, singing sad songs. All the animals and trees were moved by his music. Nothing could console him.

Postea, Orpheus a Bacchantibus, furentibus feminis Dionysi sacris, necatus est. Caput eius, adhuc canens, ad Lesbos insulam portatum est. Etiam post mortem, cantus Orphei audiebatur.

Later, Orpheus was killed by the Bacchants, frenzied women in the service of Dionysus. His head, still singing, was carried to the island of Lesbos. Even after death, the song of Orpheus was heard.

Musae, deae artium, Orphei reliquias sepelierunt. "Orpheus," dixerunt Musae, "tuus cantus in corde nostro semper manebit."

The Muses, goddesses of the arts, buried the remains of Orpheus. "Orpheus," said the Muses, "your song will always remain in our hearts."

Orpheus, post mortem, ad Elysium campos, locum beatum, pervenit. Ibi, tandem, Orpheus et Eurydice iterum iuncti sunt. In Elysium campis, in pace et amore, Orpheus et Eurydice aeternum sunt.

After death, Orpheus arrived at the Elysian Fields, a place of bliss. There, at last, Orpheus and Eurydice were reunited. In the Elysian Fields, in peace and love, Orpheus and Eurydice are together forever.

Sic finitur fabula Orphei et Eurydices, fabula de amore immenso, de arte musicae, et de spe et dolore in amore. Orpheus, per carmina sua, semper in memoria hominum manebit, exemplar amoris veri et artis magnae.

Thus ends the story of Orpheus and Eurydice, a tale of immense love, of the art of music, and of hope and sorrow in love. Orpheus, through his songs, will always remain in the memory of humanity, an example of true love and great art.

Bacchus et Pentheus

In antiqua Graecia, Bacchus, deus vini et festivitatum, ad Thebas, urbem magnam et pulchram, venit.

In ancient Greece, Bacchus, the god of wine and festivals, came to Thebes, a great and beautiful city.

Bacchus, cum thyrsis et coronis, festum magnum parabat. Multi Thebani Bacchum colebant et cum eo festum celebrabant.

Bacchus, with his thyrsus and garlands, prepared a great festival. Many Thebans worshiped Bacchus and celebrated the festival with him.

Pentheus, tamen, rex Thebarum, Bacchum non colebat. "Cur homines hoc deo falso et vinum bibenti colunt?" iratus Pentheus dixit. "Non permitto hanc insaniam in mea urbe!"

However, Pentheus, the king of Thebes, did not worship Bacchus. "Why do people worship this false god who drinks wine?" said the angry Pentheus. "I will not allow this madness in my city!"

Bacchus, audito Pentheum se non colente, consilium cepit. "Pentheus me non colit," dixit Bacchus, "sed ego eum docebo quis sum."

Bacchus, upon hearing that Pentheus did not worship him, made a plan. "Pentheus does not honor me," said Bacchus, "but I will teach him who I am."

Bacchus, arte sua, Pentheum in montem duxit ubi Bacchantes, sectatores Bacchi, festum celebrabant. "Vide, Pentheu," inquit Bacchus, "mei sectatores sunt ubique. Eorum numerus magis magisque crescit."

Bacchus, using his power, led Pentheus to a mountain where the Bacchantes, Bacchus' followers, were celebrating a festival. "Look, Pentheus," said Bacchus, "my followers are everywhere. Their numbers are growing more and more."

Pentheus, in arboris cacumine celatus, Bacchantes spectabat. "Insania est!" murmuravit Pentheus. "Oportet me hanc insaniam prohibere."

Pentheus, hidden in the treetop, watched the Bacchantes. "This is madness!" murmured Pentheus. "I must stop this insanity."

Sed Bacchantes, Pentheum in arbore celatum videntes, irati sunt. "Ecce! Homo nos spectat!" exclamaverunt. "Puniamus eum!"

But the Bacchantes, seeing Pentheus hidden in the tree, became angry. "Look! A man is watching us!" they exclaimed. "Let's punish him!"

Bacchantes, furore motae, ad arborem cucurrerunt et Pentheum de arbore traxerunt. In furore, Pentheum discerperunt. Mater eius, Agave, etiam inter Bacchantes erat, furore captata.

The Bacchantes, driven by frenzy, ran to the tree and dragged Pentheus down. In their fury, they tore Pentheus apart. His mother, Agave, was also among the Bacchantes, overcome by madness.

Agave, caput Penthei in manibus tenens, ad urbem rediit. "Vide, fili mei caput!" in foro clamavit. "Victoriam de hoste nostro habemus!"

Agave, holding Pentheus' head in her hands, returned to the city. "Look, my son's head!" she shouted in the marketplace. "We have victory over our enemy!"

Cives Thebani, horrore affecti, ad Agavem accesserunt. "Agave," dixerunt, "hoc est caput Penthei, filii tui!" Agave, veritatem intellegens, subito lugebat. "O me miseram!" clamavit. "Quid feci?!"

The Theban citizens, horrified, approached Agave. "Agave," they said, "this is the head of Pentheus, your son!" Agave, realizing the truth, suddenly began to grieve. "Oh, miserable me!" she cried. "What have I done?!"

Bacchus, Thebas spectans, Penthei mortem vindicavit. "Pentheus me spernebat," dixit Bacchus, "nunc omnes sciant potentiam meam."

Bacchus, watching Thebes, avenged Pentheus' death. "Pentheus despised me," said Bacchus, "now everyone will know my power."

Bacchus, iratus, Thebas maledixit. Sed eius cultus per Graeciam diffundebatur. Homines Bacchum colebant et eius festa celebrabant.

Bacchus, in his anger, cursed Thebes. But his worship spread throughout Greece. People worshiped Bacchus and celebrated his festivals.

Pentheus, exemplum impietatis et superbiae, in memoria hominum manebat. Bacchus, interea, in templo suo honoratus erat.

Pentheus, an example of impiety and pride, remained in the memory of people. Meanwhile, Bacchus was honored in his temple.

Sic finitur fabula de Baccho et Pentheo, de deorum ira, et de mortalium superbia. Bacchus, deus vini, in Graeciae cultura magni momenti erat, et Thebae, propter Penthei mortem, infamiae notae sunt.

Thus ends the story of Bacchus and Pentheus, about the wrath of the gods and the pride of mortals. Bacchus, the god of wine, was of great importance in Greek culture, and Thebes became known for its infamy due to Pentheus' death.

Arachne et Minerva

In Lydia, antiqua regione, erat puella nomine Arachne.

In Lydia, an ancient region, there was a girl named Arachne.

Arachne in arte texendi peritissima erat. Textilia eius tam pulchra erant ut omnes qui ea viderent mirarentur. "Ecce," dicebant homines, "quam pulchra sunt Arachnis textilia! Num deae ipsae melius texere possunt?"

Arachne was highly skilled in the art of weaving. Her textiles were so beautiful that all who saw them marveled. "Look," people said, "how beautiful Arachne's textiles are! Could the goddesses themselves weave better?"

Fama Arachnis ad Minervam, texendi deam, pervenit. Minerva, dea sapientiae et artis texendi, de fama Arachnis audivit et ad eam venire constituit. Sub forma vetulae ad Arachnem accessit. "Iuvenis," inquit Minerva, "artis tuae perita es, sed cave ne te superbia decipiat. Semper deos honora."

The fame of Arachne reached Minerva, the goddess of weaving. Minerva, the goddess of wisdom and the art of weaving, heard of Arachne's fame and decided to visit her. In the form of an old woman, she approached Arachne. "Young one," said Minerva, "you are skilled in your art, but be careful not to be deceived by pride. Always honor the gods."

Arachne, Minervam non agnoscens, risit. "Deae me non metuunt," inquit Arachne. "Si quae dea me provocare audet, cum ea in certamine texendi contendam."

Arachne, not recognizing Minerva, laughed. "The goddesses do not frighten me," said Arachne. "If any goddess dares to challenge me, I will compete with her in a weaving contest."

Minerva, forma vetulae deposita, veram suam formam revelavit. "Ego sum Minerva," inquit. "Tuam provocationem accipio et tecum certabo."

Minerva, dropping the form of the old woman, revealed her true form. "I am Minerva," she said. "I accept your challenge, and I will compete with you."

Arachne et Minerva, ad telas stantes, coeperunt texere. Arachne textilia cum historiis deorum texebat, quae deorum vitiis narrabant. Minerva autem in sua tela se ipsam et alios deos virtutibus praeditos depinxit.

Arachne and Minerva, standing at their looms, began to weave. Arachne wove textiles with stories about the gods, highlighting their flaws. Minerva, however, depicted herself and the other gods endowed with virtues in her tapestry.

Cum texendi opus finitum est, omnes qui aderant mirabantur. Textilia utriusque erant mira. Sed Minerva, videns quod Arachne in tela sua deos irriserat, irata est. Minerva Arachnen verberavit.

When the weaving was finished, all who were present were amazed. The textiles of both were magnificent. But Minerva, seeing that Arachne had mocked the gods in her tapestry, became angry. Minerva struck Arachne.

Arachne, dolore et pudore affecta, se suspendit. Minerva, misericordia mota, dixit: "Vive, Arachne, sed monitum tene. Semper texito, sed nunc in aliam formam mutaberis." Arachne in araneam mutata est.

Arachne, affected by pain and shame, hanged herself. Minerva, moved by mercy, said: "Live, Arachne, but heed this warning. Always weave, but now you will be changed into another form." Arachne was transformed into a spider.

Arachne, nunc aranea, adhuc texere pergit. Eius historia in arte texendi semper memoratur. Haec fabula docet nos superbiae pericula et deorum potentiam.

Arachne, now a spider, continues to weave. Her story is always remembered in the art of weaving. This story teaches us about the dangers of pride and the power of the gods.

Eius exemplum docet artis excellentiam et superbiae periculum. Sic finitur fabula Arachne, quae, ob superbiam suam, in araneam a Minerva, sapientiae et artis deae, mutata est. Arachne etiam nunc in tela sua mirabilia texere pergit, aranea facta, monens nos omnes de humilitate et reverentia erga deos.

Her example teaches the excellence of art and the danger of pride. Thus ends the story of Arachne, who, because of her pride, was turned into a spider by Minerva, the goddess of wisdom and art. Arachne still continues to weave her wonders in her web, as a spider, reminding us all of humility and reverence toward the gods.

Niobe et Liberorum Eius Interitus

In antiqua urbe Thebis, Niobe, regina pulcherrima, vivebat.

In the ancient city of Thebes, Niobe, a most beautiful queen, lived.

Multos filios filiasque habebat, et superbia plena erat. "Videte," Niobe saepe dicebat, "quot filios et filias pulchras habeo. Nulla in hac terra mihi similis est, ne Latonae quidem, Apollinis et Dianae matris."

She had many sons and daughters, and was full of pride. "Look," Niobe often said, "how many sons and beautiful daughters I have. No one on this earth is like me, not even Latona, the mother of Apollo and Diana."

Latona, dea veneranda, haec verba audivit et irata est. "Quomodo mortalis me se superiorem praedicat?" inquit. Filios suos, Apollinem et Dianam, ad Niobem misit. "Punite eam pro superbia sua," Latona imperavit.

Latona, the revered goddess, heard these words and became angry. "How does a mortal claim to be superior to me?" she said. She sent her children, Apollo and Diana, to Niobe. "Punish her for her pride," Latona commanded.

Apollo et Diana, sagittis suis potentes, ad Thebas venerunt. Filii Niobes, nihil mali suspicantes, in campo ludebant. Subito, Apollo sagittis suis unum post alterum filios Niobes necavit. Diana, non minus irata, filias Niobes sagittis suis interfecit.

Apollo and Diana, powerful with their arrows, came to Thebes. Niobe's sons, suspecting no harm, were playing in the field. Suddenly, Apollo, with his arrows, killed Niobe's sons one by one. Diana, no less angry, killed Niobe's daughters with her arrows.

Niobe, videns filios suos mortuos, dolore affecta est. "O filii mei," clamavit Niobe, "quid feci ut hoc patiar?" Lacrimas multas effudit, sed deorum ira non placata est.

Niobe, seeing her children dead, was overwhelmed with grief. "Oh, my children," Niobe cried, "what have I done to suffer this?" She shed many tears, but the anger of the gods was not appeased.

Amphion, Niobes maritus, cum filiorum corporibus inventus est. Ipse se occiderat, dolore superatus. Thebani, urbis incolae, filios et filias Niobes sepelierunt. Niobe autem, adhuc lacrimans, in saxum mutata est.

Amphion, Niobe's husband, was found among the bodies of his sons. He had killed himself, overcome by grief. The Thebans, citizens of the city, buried Niobe's sons and daughters. But Niobe, still weeping, was transformed into a stone.

Saxum Niobes in monte Sipylus videtur, et lacrimae eius adhuc fluunt. Niobis superbia et dolor exempla sunt. Haec fabula docet nos deorum reverentiam et superbiae pericula.

The stone of Niobe is seen on Mount Sipylus, and her tears still flow. Niobe's pride and sorrow serve as examples. This story teaches us about reverence for the gods and the dangers of pride.

Niobe, quondam regina potens et superba, nunc saxum est, memoria perpetua superbiae et doloris. Filii eius, quondam vivi et laeti, nunc in tumulis iacent, monitum triste superbiae maternae.

Niobe, once a powerful and proud queen, is now a stone, a lasting memory of pride and grief. Her sons, once alive and joyful, now lie in tombs, a sad reminder of a mother's pride.

Dei, in fabula Niobes, vindictam in superbos sumunt. Apollo et Diana, non solum de pulchritudine et artibus, sed etiam de ira et poena, memores sunt.

The gods, in Niobe's story, take vengeance on the proud. Apollo and Diana are remembered not only for beauty and the arts, but also for their anger and punishment.

Niobe, cum filiis suis, in mythologia Graeca memorabilis est. Eorum historia, per saecula narrata, nos monet ne superbia nos capiat et ne deos spernamus.

Niobe, with her children, is memorable in Greek mythology. Their story, told through the ages, reminds us not to be overtaken by pride and not to scorn the gods.

Sic finit tristis historia Niobes, reginae Thebarum, quae, propter superbiam suam et verba temeraria, omnia perdiderat. Eius dolor et poena in historia Graeca semper memorentur, exemplum aeternum deorum potentiae et humanorum limitum.

Thus ends the sad story of Niobe, queen of Thebes, who, because of her pride and reckless words, lost everything. Her grief and punishment are forever remembered in Greek history, an eternal example of the gods' power and human limitations.

Marsyas et Apollo

In antiquis Graeciae temporibus, Marsyas, satyrus ludens et hilaris, forte tibiam in silva invenit.

In ancient times in Greece, Marsyas, a playful and joyful satyr, by chance found a flute in the forest.

Haec tibia a dea Athena relicta erat. Marsyas, tibiam tollens, arte musica excellere coepit. Cuncti qui eum audiebant, mirabantur, "Ecce," dicebant, "quam mirabiliter Marsyas canit!"

This flute had been left by the goddess Athena. Marsyas, taking up the flute, began to excel in the art of music. Everyone who heard him marveled, saying, "Look how wonderfully Marsyas plays!"

Apollo, deus musicae et citharae peritus, de Marsya audivit. "Quis est hic qui se me aequare audet?" interrogavit Apollo.

Apollo, decernere volens quis melior in musica esset, ad Marsyam venit. "Ego te provocare audeo," dixit Apollo. "Certemus et videamus quis melior musicus sit."

Apollo, the god of music and skilled with the lyre, heard about Marsyas. "Who is this who dares to equal me?" Apollo asked. Wishing to decide who was better in music, Apollo came to Marsyas. "I dare to challenge you," said Apollo. "Let us compete and see who is the better musician."

Marsyas, audaciter, provocationem accepit. "Certemus," inquit Marsyas. "Gaudeo hac occasione mecum cum te, deo musicae, contendere." Certamen igitur statutum est. Marsyas tibiam, Apollo citharam, cecinerunt. Musica eorum silvas et montes implevit.

Marsyas, boldly, accepted the challenge. "Let us compete," said Marsyas. "I am glad for this opportunity to contend with you, the god of music." So the contest was set. Marsyas played the flute, Apollo the lyre. Their music filled the forests and mountains.

Iudices, quorum inter erant Musae, audiebant et iudicandum erat. Postquam utrique finem fecerunt, iudices Apollinem victorem declaraverunt. "Apollo," dixerunt, "musica tua nos magis movit. Tu es victor."

The judges, among whom were the Muses, listened and had to make a decision. After both had finished, the judges declared Apollo the victor. "Apollo," they said, "your music moved us more. You are the winner."

Apollo, victor, ad Marsyam accessit. "Tu me provocabas," inquit. "Nunc poenam tuam dabis." Apollo, iratus et superbus, Marsyam vivus excoriavit. E loco ubi Marsyas poenam dabat, flumina ex sanguine eius fluxerunt.

Apollo, as the victor, approached Marsyas. "You challenged me," he said. "Now you will pay your penalty." Apollo, angry and proud, flayed Marsyas alive. From the place where Marsyas suffered, rivers flowed from his blood.

Marsyas, licet victus et crudeli poena affectus, in arte musica semper memoratur. Eius audacia, contra deum ipsum certare ausus, in mythologia Graeca exemplum est. Apollo autem, per hanc fabulam, severitatem suam et potestatem ostendit.

Marsyas, though defeated and affected by cruel punishment, is always remembered in the art of music. His boldness in daring to challenge a god himself is an example in Greek mythology. Apollo, however, through this story, showed his severity and power.

Haec fabula docet nos deorum potestatem et mortalium audaciam. Marsyas, licet peritus musicus, contra deum contendere non potuit sine gravi poena. Apollo, potens et iratus, in arte saepe depictus est, exemplar deorum irae et iustitiae.

This story teaches us about the power of the gods and the boldness of mortals. Marsyas, although a skilled musician, could not challenge a god without severe punishment. Apollo, powerful and angry, is often depicted in art as an example of divine wrath and justice.

Sic finitur fabula Marsyae et Apollonis, fabula de audacia, musica, et deorum potestate. Marsyas, in mythologia Graeca memorabilis, semper monitum praebet de limitibus humanis et respectu deorum. Apollo, per hanc historiam, hominibus docet de reverentia quae debetur deis et de periculis superbiae et audaciae.

Thus ends the story of Marsyas and Apollo, a tale of boldness, music, and divine power. Marsyas, memorable in Greek mythology, always serves as a reminder of human limits and respect for the gods. Through this story, Apollo teaches humans about the reverence due to the gods and the dangers of pride and audacity.

Pelias et Medea

In Thessalia, regno Graeciae antiquae, Pelias, Iasonis avunculus, imperabat.

In Thessaly, an ancient kingdom of Greece, Pelias, the uncle of Jason, ruled.

Pelias, vir astutus et potens, Iasoni, iuveni forti et audaci, imperavit ut vellus aureum, quod in Colchis erat, reportaret. "Si vellus aureum mihi adferes," dixit Pelias, "tibi regnum dabo."

Pelias, a cunning and powerful man, commanded Jason, a strong and daring young man, to bring back the golden fleece, which was in Colchis. "If you bring me the golden fleece," said Pelias, "I will give you the kingdom."

Iason, arduum opus suscipiens, ad Colchis navigavit. Ibi, Medea, regis filia et maga perita, Iasonem vidit et statim eum amavit. "Quis est ille iuvenis tam fortis et pulcher?" se interrogavit Medea.

Jason, undertaking the difficult task, sailed to Colchis. There, Medea, the daughter of the king and a skilled sorceress, saw Jason and immediately fell in love with him. "Who is that young man so strong and handsome?" Medea asked herself.

Medea, amore Iasonis capta, ad eum accessit. "Iason," inquit Medea, "ego sum Medea, maga. Auxilium tibi polliceor in quaerendo vello aureo." Iason, Medeae auxilio laetus, consensit.

Medea, captivated by her love for Jason, approached him. "Jason," said Medea, "I am Medea, a sorceress. I promise to help you in seeking the golden fleece." Jason, pleased with Medea's help, agreed.

Cum arte magica Medeae, Iason vellus aureum cepit. Iason et Medea, vello aureo potiti, ad Thessaliam navigaverunt. Pelias, vellus videns, gaudebat, sed regnum Iasoni reddere noluit.

With Medea's magical skills, Jason obtained the golden fleece. Jason and Medea, having gained the fleece, sailed back to Thessaly. Pelias, seeing the fleece, rejoiced but refused to return the kingdom to Jason.

Medea, irata Peliae perfidia, arte sua eum interfecit. Nocte, Peliam somno profundo oppressum venenis suis interfecit. Mane facto, Peliae filiae patrem mortuum invenerunt et magno dolore affectae sunt.

Medea, angry at Pelias' treachery, killed him with her magic. During the night, she killed Pelias, who was overcome by deep sleep, with her poisons. In the morning, Pelias' daughters found their father dead and were overwhelmed with great sorrow.

Acastus, Peliae filius, Iasonem et Medeam ex urbe expulit. "Proditionem vestram non tolerabo," inquit Acastus. "Exite ex Thessalia!" Iason et Medea, urbe expulsi, Corinthum fugerunt.

Acastus, the son of Pelias, expelled Jason and Medea from the city. "I will not tolerate your treachery," said Acastus. "Leave Thessaly!" Jason and Medea, expelled from the city, fled to Corinth.

Iasonis et Medeae fabula est de amore, proditione, et magia. Medea, maga potens, pro amore Iasonis omnia facere parata erat. Iason, vellus aureum quaerens, in amoris et proditorum rete incidit.

The story of Jason and Medea is one of love, betrayal, and magic. Medea, a powerful sorceress, was ready to do anything for her love for Jason. Jason, seeking the golden fleece, fell into a web of love and betrayal.

Medea, in mythologia Graeca, maga potens et periculosa est. Eius figura in fabulis et carminibus antiquis saepe apparet, exemplar potentiae magicae et amoris ardentis.

Medea, in Greek mythology, is a powerful and dangerous sorceress. Her figure often appears in ancient tales and poems, as an example of magical power and burning love.

Sic finitur fabula Peliae, Iasonis, et Medeae. Narratio haec de amoris potestate, magiae periculo, et humanorum animorum varietate est. Medea et Iason, per saecula, in memoria hominum manent, exempla amoris fortis et fatalis.

Thus ends the story of Pelias, Jason, and Medea. This tale is about the power of love, the danger of magic, and the complexity of human emotions. Medea and Jason remain in human memory through the ages, examples of strong and fateful love.

Tereus, Procne, et Philomela

In regno Thraciae, Tereus, rex fortis et potens, regnabat.

In the kingdom of Thrace, Tereus, a strong and powerful king, reigned.

Uxorem habebat nomine Procnen, pulchram et nobilem feminam. Procne et Tereus filium parvum, Ityn nomine, habebant. Procne sororem habebat nomine Philomelam, quae in alia urbe vivebat.

He had a wife named Procne, a beautiful and noble woman. Procne and Tereus had a young son named Itys. Procne had a sister named Philomela, who lived in another city.

Unum diem, Procne Tereum rogavit ut Philomelam ad Thraciam invitaret. "Desidero sororem meam videre," inquit Procne. Tereus, consentiens, ad urbem Philomelae navigavit.

One day, Procne asked Tereus to invite Philomela to Thrace. "I wish to see my sister," said Procne. Tereus, agreeing, sailed to Philomela's city.

Cum Philomelam vidit, Tereus eam statim amavit, sed non honesto amore. Philomelam decepit et eam ad Thraciam secum duxit. In silvis solis, Philomelam rapuit et crudeliter tractavit.

When he saw Philomela, Tereus immediately desired her, but not with honorable love. He deceived her and took her with him to Thrace. In a lonely forest, he raped Philomela and treated her cruelly.

Philomela, dolore et ira plena, Tereum accusavit. "Cur me hoc fecisti?" clamavit. "Soror mea hoc sciet!" Tereus, timens veritatem revelari, Philomelae linguam crudeliter abscidit.

Philomela, filled with pain and anger, accused Tereus. "Why have you done this to me?" she cried. "My sister will know!" Tereus, fearing the truth would be revealed, cruelly cut out Philomela's tongue.

Philomela, loqui non valens, telam texuit. In tela, totam historiam suam scripsit. Tela ad Procnen misit, quae veritatem intellexit. Procne, fabulam legens, ira et dolore affecta est.

Unable to speak, Philomela wove a tapestry. In the tapestry, she told her entire story. She sent the tapestry to Procne, who understood the truth. Procne, reading the tale, was filled with anger and sorrow.

Procne, vindictam cupiens, filium suum Ityn interfecit. Itys, innocens puer, a matre sua occisus est. Procne et Philomela partes corporis Itys Tereui apposuerunt.

Desiring revenge, Procne killed her son Itys. Itys, an innocent boy, was slain by his own mother. Procne and Philomela served parts of Itys' body to Tereus.

Tereus, cena edens, de filio suo interrogavit. "Ubi est Itys?" inquit. Procne et Philomela veritatem revelaverunt. Tereus, horrenda veritate intellegendo, iratus est et gladium sumpsit.

While eating the meal, Tereus asked about his son. "Where is Itys?" he asked. Procne and Philomela revealed the truth. Realizing the horrifying truth, Tereus became enraged and grabbed his sword.

Dei, scelera videndo, Tereum in upupam, Procnen in hirundinem, Philomelam in lusciniam mutaverunt. Tereus, Procne, et Philomela, nunc aves, volaverunt, tristes historias suas portantes.

The gods, seeing these crimes, transformed Tereus into a hoopoe, Procne into a swallow, and Philomela into a nightingale. Tereus, Procne, and Philomela, now birds, flew away, carrying their sad stories with them.

Fabula Terei, Procnes, et Philomelae est de crudelitate, vindicta, et amore fraterno. Eorum historia in mythologia Graeca memorabilis est, exemplum amoris periculosi et irae terribilis.

The story of Tereus, Procne, and Philomela is one of cruelty, revenge, and sibling love. Their tale is memorable in Greek mythology, an example of dangerous love and terrible anger.

In arte et litteris, fabula saepe tractata est. Aves, quae olim fuerunt Tereus, Procne, et Philomela, in fabulis et carminibus saepe apparebant, monentes nos de periculis crudelitatis et vindictae.

In art and literature, the tale has often been explored. The birds, once Tereus, Procne, and Philomela, frequently appear in stories and poems, warning us of the dangers of cruelty and revenge.

Sic finitur tristis historia Terei, Procnes, et Philomelae. Eorum casus nos docet de potentia amoris et periculis irae in humanis cordibus. In mythologia Graeca, haec fabula semper monitum est de humanis passionibus et deorum iudiciis.

Thus ends the tragic story of Tereus, Procne, and Philomela. Their fate teaches us about the power of love and the dangers of rage in human hearts. In Greek mythology, this tale is always a warning of human passions and divine judgments.

157

Boreas et Orithyia

In antiquis Graeciae temporibus, Boreas, ventorum rex potens et vehemens, in Orithyiam, Athenarum regis filiam, amore incidit.

In ancient times in Greece, Boreas, the powerful and fierce king of the winds, fell in love with Orithyia, the daughter of the king of Athens.

Orithyia, pulchra et grata, per campos ludebat, nescia amoris Boreae.

Orithyia, beautiful and graceful, was playing in the fields, unaware of Boreas' love.

Boreas, amore Orithyiae captus, diu eam observavit. "O Orithyia," in corde suo dicebat, "tu es pulcherrima omnium. Te amare non possum desistere." Sed timuit ne amor eius non rediretur.

Boreas, captivated by love for Orithyia, watched her for a long time. "O Orithyia," he said in his heart, "you are the most beautiful of all. I cannot stop loving you." But he feared that his love would not be returned.

Tandem, Boreas non amplius se continere potuit. Ventis suis validis, Orithyiam rapuit et ad Thraciam, suam patriam, portavit. Orithyia, territa et confusa, quid ageret nesciebat.

At last, Boreas could no longer contain himself. With his powerful winds, he carried off Orithyia and took her to Thrace, his homeland. Orithyia, frightened and confused, did not know what to do.

In Thracia, Boreas Orithyiae suum amorem declaravit. "Orithyia, te amo," inquit Boreas. "Mea regina esse velim." Orithyia, primo territa, mox Boreae amorem accepit, nam et ipsa cor eius movebat.

In Thrace, Boreas declared his love to Orithyia. "Orithyia, I love you," said Boreas. "I wish you to be my queen." At first terrified, Orithyia soon accepted Boreas' love, for she too was moved by his heart.

Ex eorum amore duo filii nati sunt, Calais et Zetes, gemini cum alis pulchris. Filii, alis volantes, in fabulis heroicis noti facti sunt. Argonautis, in quaerendo vellere aureo, auxilium tulerunt.

From their love, two sons were born, Calais and Zetes, twins with beautiful wings. The sons, flying with their wings, became famous in heroic tales. They aided the Argonauts in their quest for the Golden Fleece.

Boreas, rex ventorum, tempestates et ventos regebat. Orithyia, uxor fida, eum in regno suo adiuvabat. Eorum amor in mythologia Graeca celebratus est, exemplum amoris inter deum naturae et mortalem.

Boreas, king of the winds, ruled over storms and winds. Orithyia, his faithful wife, helped him in his kingdom. Their love was celebrated in Greek mythology, an example of love between a god of nature and a mortal.

Boreas, in arte et poesi, saepe depictus est, potens et terribilis, sed etiam amans. Eorum historia nos docet de potestate naturae et deorum, necnon de amoris miraculis.

Boreas, in art and poetry, was often depicted as powerful and terrifying, but also loving. Their story teaches us about the power of nature and the gods, as well as the miracles of love.

Calais et Zetes, filii eorum, in multis fabulis heroicis apparuerunt, exempla virtutis et fortitudinis. Eorum historiae in multas culturas Graeciae antiquae penetraverunt.

Calais and Zetes, their sons, appeared in many heroic stories, as examples of virtue and strength. Their stories spread into many cultures of ancient Greece.

Fabula Boreae et Orithyiae est de naturae potestatibus, amoribus deorum, et miraculis quae ex his nascuntur. In cultu Graeco, Boreas et Orithyia honore magno habiti sunt.

The story of Boreas and Orithyia is about the powers of nature, the loves of gods, and the miracles that arise from these. In Greek culture, Boreas and Orithyia were held in great honor.

Boreas, propter suam vim et potestatem, in antiqua religione Graeca reveritus est. Orithyia, exemplar feminae mortalis quae deum amavit, in memoria hominum manet.

Boreas, because of his strength and power, was revered in ancient Greek religion. Orithyia, an example of a mortal woman who loved a god, remains in the memory of people.

Sic finitur fabula Boreae et Orithyiae, regis ventorum et Athenarum regis filiae. Eorum amor, per saecula, in carminibus et fabulis narratus est, monens nos de potentia naturae et de mirabilibus quae in mundo nostro eveniunt.

Thus ends the story of Boreas and Orithyia, king of the winds and the daughter of the king of Athens. Their love, over the centuries, has been told in poems and tales, reminding us of the power of nature and the wonders that happen in our world.

Alcithoe et Minyades

In antiqua Graecia, in urbe Thebis, vixerunt tres sorores, Alcithoe et duae sorores eius, quae Minyades appellabantur.

In ancient Greece, in the city of Thebes, there lived three sisters, Alcithoe and her two sisters, who were called the Minyads.

Hae tres, diversae a ceteris civibus, Bacchum, deum vini et festivitatum, non colebant. Dum tota urbs Bacchi festa celebrabat, illae domi manebant et lanam texebant.

These three, unlike the other citizens, did not worship Bacchus, the god of wine and festivities. While the whole city celebrated Bacchus' festival, they stayed at home and wove wool.

"Cur nos Bacchum colere debemus?" Alcithoe saepe interrogavit. "Nonne nostra opera in lanificio nobis satis est?" Sorores consentiebant et ita Bacchi festis neglegebant.

162

"Why should we worship Bacchus?" Alcithoe often asked. "Isn't our work in weaving enough for us?" Her sisters agreed, and so they neglected Bacchus' festivals.

Bacchus, deorum inter eos potens et vindicativus, de hac neglecta iratus est. "Quomodo mortales me spernere audent?" inquit Bacchus. "Eas pro contemptu meo puniam!"

Bacchus, a powerful and vengeful god among the gods, was angry about this neglect. "How dare mortals scorn me?" said Bacchus. "I will punish them for their contempt!"

Subito, dum Alcithoe et sorores lanas texebant, mira transformatio accidit. Tres sorores in vespertiliones, nocturnas volucres, mutatae sunt. Territae et confusae, ad cavernas fugerunt.

Suddenly, while Alcithoe and her sisters were weaving, a strange transformation occurred. The three sisters were turned into bats, nocturnal creatures. Frightened and confused, they fled to caves.

Etiam ut vespertiliones, Alcithoe et sorores texere pergebant, textilia mira et obscura facientes. "Videte," dicebant homines, "quomodo etiam in hac forma miserae sorores texere non cessant!"

Even as bats, Alcithoe and her sisters continued to weave, creating strange and dark textiles. "Look," said the people, "how even in this miserable form the sisters do not stop weaving!"

Eorum historia in Thebis et per Graeciam narrata est, exemplum superbiae et deorum poenae. "Bacchus," dicebant cives, "deus est non spernendus. Eius iram videte in fato miserarum Minyadum."

Their story was told in Thebes and throughout Greece, as an example of pride and divine punishment. "Bacchus," the citizens said, "is a god not to be scorned. See his wrath in the fate of the wretched Minyads."

Fabula Minyadum in arte Graeca et litteris perpetua est. Vespertiliones, quae olim Alcithoe et sorores fuerunt, in picturis et carminibus saepe apparebant, monentes de periculis superbiae et contemptus deorum.

The tale of the Minyads endures in Greek art and literature. The bats, who were once Alcithoe and her sisters, often appeared in paintings and poems, warning of the dangers of pride and disdain for the gods.

Alcithoe et sorores, in cavernis habitantes, in silvis et montibus errabant. Nocte volabant, texebant, et tristem fatum suum lugebant.

Alcithoe and her sisters, living in caves, wandered in the forests and mountains. At night they flew, wove, and mourned their sad fate.

Casus earum exemplar est deorum irae et potentiae. Bacchus, per hanc historiam, docet homines de reverentia quae debetur divinis et de periculis quae sequuntur si hoc neglegitur.

Their downfall is an example of the wrath and power of the gods. Through this story, Bacchus teaches people about the reverence due to the divine and the dangers that follow if this is neglected.

Sic finitur tristis sed docta fabula Alcithoe et Minyadum. Eorum memoria in cultu Graeco manet, monens nos omnes de respectu deorum et de poena quae sequi potest si hoc oblita est.

Thus ends the sad but instructive tale of Alcithoe and the Minyads. Their memory remains in Greek culture, reminding us all of the respect owed to the gods and the punishment that may follow if it is forgotten.

Mars et Venus

In Olympo, domo deorum, Mars, bellorum deus fortis et audax, secreto Venerem, amoris deam pulchram, amabat.

In Olympus, the home of the gods, Mars, the bold and strong god of war, secretly loved Venus, the beautiful goddess of love.

Venus, quae Vulcani, fabri dei, uxor erat, etiam Martem favebat. Amor eorum, inter deos secretus, apud omnes in Olympo latebat.

Venus, who was the wife of Vulcan, the god of smiths, also favored Mars. Their love, a secret among the gods, was hidden from everyone in Olympus.

Vulcanus, Veneris maritus, deorum faber peritus, suspicionem habebat. "Cur Venus, uxor mea, saepe abest?" cogitabat. Ingenio suo et arte fabrili, rete mirabile fabricavit, quod invisibile et tenacissimum erat.

Vulcan, the husband of Venus and a skilled smith among the gods, grew suspicious. "Why is my wife, Venus, often absent?" he thought. With his skill and craft, he forged a miraculous net, invisible and very strong.

Dum Mars et Venus in cubiculo Veneris amorem suum colebant, rete Vulcani super eos cecidit. In rete capti, movere non poterant. "Heu!" exclamavit Venus. "Capti sumus!"

While Mars and Venus were in Venus' chamber enjoying their love, Vulcan's net fell over them. Caught in the net, they could not move. "Alas!" cried Venus. "We are trapped!"

Vulcanus, iratus et triumphans, ad eos venit. "Ecce," inquit Vulcanus, "uxor mea et amator eius!" Ceteri dei ad spectaculum venerunt, et risus magnus in Olympo fuit.

Vulcan, angry and triumphant, came to them. "Behold," said Vulcan, "my wife and her lover!" The other gods came to see the spectacle, and great laughter filled Olympus.

Venus, pudore affecta, caput demisit. "O me miseram," susurravit. "Nunc omnes de nostro amore secreto scient." Mars, iratus, Vulcanum aspexit et dixit: "Cur nos sic dedecoras? Amor noster secretus erat!"

Venus, filled with shame, lowered her head. "Oh, miserable me," she whispered. "Now everyone will know about our secret love." Mars, angry, looked at Vulcan and said: "Why do you disgrace us like this? Our love was secret!"

Dei ad eos ridebant. "Ecce Mars et Venus!" clamabant. "Amores eorum aperti sunt!" Fabula de adulterio Martis et Veneris per totum Olympum diffusa est.

The gods laughed at them. "Look, Mars and Venus!" they shouted. "Their love has been revealed!" The story of Mars and Venus' affair spread throughout Olympus.

Venus et Mars, in arte et poesi, saepe depicti sunt. Historia eorum de amore secreto et decepto est fabula. Amor eorum exemplum est amoris prohibiti et passionis secreti.

Venus and Mars are often depicted in art and poetry. Their story is a tale of secret and deceived love. Their love is an example of forbidden love and hidden passion.

Vulcanus, per hanc fabulam, ingenium et artificium suum ostendit. Rete eius, ingeniose fabricatum, amores secretos revelavit. Fabula haec deorum humanisque passionibus est, demonstrans etiam deos passionibus humanis subiectos esse.

Vulcan, through this story, showed his cleverness and skill. His ingeniously crafted net revealed the secret love. This tale is about both divine and human passions, showing that even the gods are subject to human-like desires.

Mars et Venus, noti in mythologia Graeca, exempla sunt deorum mores et ingenia. Eorum historia nos docet de amoris potestate et de periculis deceptionis in amoribus.

Mars and Venus, known in Greek mythology, are examples of the behaviors and nature of the gods. Their story teaches us about the power of love and the dangers of deceit in relationships.

Sic finitur fabula Martis et Veneris, deorum amantium. Eorum amor, licet secretus, per Vulcani ingenium revelatus est, monens nos de veritate quae saepe post deceptionem latet.

Thus ends the tale of Mars and Venus, the divine lovers. Their love, though secret, was revealed through Vulcan's ingenuity, reminding us that truth often follows deception.

Niobe

In antiquis temporibus, in urbe Thebis, Niobe, Amphionis uxor, regina pulchra et potens, vivebat.

In ancient times, in the city of Thebes, Niobe, the wife of Amphion, a beautiful and powerful queen, lived.

Niobe superbia magna inflata erat propter multos filios filiasque pulchros et valentes quos habebat.

Niobe was greatly filled with pride because of the many beautiful and strong sons and daughters she had.

Unum diem, cum Latonae, matris Apollinis et Dianae, festum celebraretur, Niobe inter cives stetit et dixit: "Cur Latonam, quae tantum duos liberos habet, colitis, cum ego tot filios filiasque pulchros habeo? Me potius colere debetis."

One day, when the festival of Latona, the mother of Apollo and Diana, was being celebrated, Niobe stood among the citizens and said: "Why do you worship Latona, who has only two children, when I have so many beautiful sons and daughters? You should worship me instead."

Verba Niobes ad deos pervenerunt. Latona, offensa verbis Niobis superbiae plenis, filios suos, Apollinem et Dianam, misit ad vindictam sumendam. "Punite Nioben pro superbia sua," imperavit Latona.

Niobe's words reached the gods. Latona, offended by Niobe's words filled with pride, sent her children, Apollo and Diana, to exact revenge. "Punish Niobe for her arrogance," commanded Latona.

Apollo et Diana, sagittis suis terribilibus armati, ad Thebas volaverunt. Filii Niobes, nihil mali suspicantes, in campo ludebant. Apollo, sagittis fulgentibus, filios Niobes unum post alterum necavit.

Apollo and Diana, armed with their terrible arrows, flew to Thebes. Niobe's sons, suspecting no harm, were playing in the field. Apollo, with his gleaming arrows, killed Niobe's sons one after the other.

Diana, non minus irata, sagittis suis filias Niobes interfecit. Niobe, videns filios suos mortuos, dolore affecta est. "O filii mei, filiaeque meae!" clamavit Niobe. "Quid feci ut hoc patiar?"

Diana, no less angry, killed Niobe's daughters with her arrows. Niobe, seeing her children dead, was overcome with grief. "Oh, my sons and daughters!" cried Niobe. "What have I done to deserve this?"

Lacrimis suis effusis, Niobe in saxum mutata est. Adhuc in saxo, lacrimae eius fluebant. Amphion, Niobes maritus, dolore superatus, se ipsum interfecit.

With her tears flowing, Niobe was transformed into a stone. Even as a stone, her tears continued to flow. Amphion, Niobe's husband, overwhelmed by grief, took his own life.

Fabula Niobes exemplum est superbiae et poenae. In monte Sipylus, saxum Niobes adhuc videtur, monens nos de superbia et deorum ira.

The story of Niobe is an example of pride and punishment. On Mount Sipylus, Niobe's stone can still be seen, reminding us of pride and the wrath of the gods.

Apollo et Diana, per hanc fabulam, potentiam et iram deorum demonstraverunt. Eorum actio monitum est de reverentia quae debetur deis.

Through this tale, Apollo and Diana demonstrated the power and anger of the gods. Their actions serve as a warning about the reverence that is due to the gods.

Niobe et Amphion, in mythologia Graeca, memorabiles sunt. Eorum historia de amore materno, superbia, et poena est. In arte et poesi, Niobe saepe tractata est, exemplum humani doloris et fragilitatis.

Niobe and Amphion are memorable in Greek mythology. Their story is about maternal love, pride, and punishment. In art and poetry, Niobe is often portrayed as an example of human pain and fragility.

Eius historia nos docet de potentia deorum et de fragilitate humanorum corum.

Her story teaches us about the power of the gods and the fragility of human hearts.

Sic finitur tristis sed docta fabula Niobes, reginae Thebarum, quae propter superbia sua et verba temeraria, omnia perdiderat. Eius dolor et poena in historia Graeca semper memorentur, exemplum aeternum deorum potentiae et humanorum limitum.

Thus ends the sad but instructive tale of Niobe, queen of Thebes, who lost everything due to her pride and reckless words. Her pain and punishment are always remembered in Greek history, an eternal example of the gods' power and the limits of humans.

De Pygmalione et Galatea

In antiqua insula Cypro, Pygmalion, sculptor peritus, habitabat.

On the ancient island of Cyprus, Pygmalion, a skilled sculptor, lived.

Vir erat sine uxore, nam nullo amore incidebat. Arte sua multum delectabatur et statuas miras creabat.

He was without a wife, for he had fallen in love with no one. He found great joy in his art and created marvelous statues.

Pygmalion diu in arte laborabat. Die quodam, statuam feminam ex marmore facere coepit.

Pygmalion worked long in his art. One day, he began to make a statue of a woman from marble.

Dum sculptit, forma statuae tam pulchra fiebat, ut cor Pygmalionis moveret. Statua tam realis videbatur, ut videretur posse ambulare et loqui.

As he sculpted, the form of the statue became so beautiful that it moved Pygmalion's heart. The statue looked so real that it seemed it could walk and speak.

Pygmalion, arte sua completa, statuam spectavit et suspiravit, "O si femina talis viveret!" Statua autem muta manebat.

Pygmalion, having completed his work, gazed at the statue and sighed, "Oh, if such a woman could live!" But the statue remained silent.

Pygmalion cotidie ad officinam suam redibat, statuamque spectabat et dicebat, "O quam pulchra es!" Sed statua semper silens erat.

Every day, Pygmalion returned to his workshop, looked at the statue, and said, "Oh, how beautiful you are!" But the statue was always silent.

Die festo Veneris, Pygmalion ad templum Veneris ivit. Statuas in templo spectavit, sed nulla tam pulchra erat quam sua.

On the festival of Venus, Pygmalion went to the temple of Venus. He looked at the statues in the temple, but none were as beautiful as his own.

Ad aram accessit et preces fudit, "O Venus, dea amoris et pulchritudinis, ad te venio rogatum ferens. Amorem invenire cupio. Desidero ut mea statua, quam Galateam nomino, vera femina fiat."

He approached the altar and prayed, "Oh Venus, goddess of love and beauty, I come to you with a request. I long to find love. I wish for my statue, which I call Galatea, to become a real woman."

Venus, dea clementissima, preces eius audivit. Pygmalion domum rediit, sperans sed non credens.

Venus, the most merciful goddess, heard his prayers. Pygmalion returned home, hoping but not believing.

Ad officinam suam venit et statuam suaviter tetigit. Subito, ad tactum eius, marmor mollescere videbatur! Pygmalion obstupuit, "Num hoc verum est?"

He went to his workshop and gently touched the statue. Suddenly, at his touch, the marble seemed to soften! Pygmalion was astonished, "Could this be real?"

Statua paulatim ad vitam venit. Oculos aperuit et Pygmalionem spectavit. Tum, mirabile dictu, risit et "Salve, artifex meus," dixit.

The statue gradually came to life. She opened her eyes and looked at Pygmalion. Then, amazingly, she smiled and said, "Greetings, my creator."

Pygmalion exultavit et exclamavit, "Venus, gratias tibi ago! Meam Galateam vivam fecisti!" Galatea eum aspexit et, "Tu me creavisti. Tibi mea vita debetur," respondit.

Pygmalion rejoiced and exclaimed, "Venus, I thank you! You have made my Galatea come alive!" Galatea looked at him and replied, "You created me. I owe my life to you."

Pygmalion et Galatea multa de arte et vita locuti sunt. Pygmalion multa narravit de insula, de arte sculpturae, de floribus et arboribus, de stellis in caelo. Galatea omnia mirabatur et de mundo novo discere cupiebat.

Pygmalion and Galatea talked about many things—art and life. Pygmalion told her about the island, the art of sculpture, the flowers and trees, and the stars in the sky. Galatea marveled at everything and longed to learn about this new world.

Pygmalion Galateam per insulam duxit. Ei flumina, montes, et campos ostendit. Galatea naturam et pulchritudinem mundi amavit.

Pygmalion led Galatea through the island. He showed her rivers, mountains, and fields. Galatea loved the beauty of nature and the world.

Dies felices transierunt. Pygmalion et Galatea in amore et amicitia vixerunt. Interdum ad litus ierunt et in arena ambulaverunt. Interdum sub stellis sedebant et de futuris somniabant.

Happy days passed. Pygmalion and Galatea lived in love and friendship. Sometimes they went to the shore and walked on the sand. Sometimes they sat under the stars and dreamed about the future.

Tandem, die quodam, Pygmalion Galateae dixit, "Mea cara Galatea, tecum semper esse volo. Meam vitam tecum coniungere cupio." Galatea risit et, "Et ego, Pygmalion. Tecum meam vitam agere eligo," respondit.

Finally, one day, Pygmalion said to Galatea, "My dear Galatea, I always want to be with you. I wish to join my life with yours." Galatea smiled and replied, "And I, Pygmalion. I choose to live my life with you."

Ita Pygmalion et Galatea in matrimonium iuncti sunt. Festa celebrata sunt, et omnes in insula laetati sunt. Dei et deae dona eis miserunt, et Venus ipsa ad nuptias venit.

So Pygmalion and Galatea were joined in marriage. Celebrations were held, and everyone on the island rejoiced. The gods and goddesses sent them gifts, and Venus herself came to the wedding.

Vita eorum beata et longa fuit. Arte, amore, et felicitate, dies suos egerunt. Et semper meminerunt quomodo amor verus et arte mirabilis eos ad vitam plenam duxerunt.

Their life was blessed and long. They spent their days in art, love, and happiness. And they always remembered how true love and wonderful art had led them to a full life.

De Ceyx et Alcyone

Ceyx, Thessaliae rex, et Alcyone, filia Aeoli, magnopere inter se amabant.

Ceyx, king of Thessaly, and Alcyone, daughter of Aeolus, loved each other deeply.

In Thessaliae regno, omnes de eorum amore sciebant. Ceyx et Alcyone semper felices erant.

In the kingdom of Thessaly, everyone knew of their love. Ceyx and Alcyone were always happy.

Sed tempore quodam, Ceyx navigare debuit. Mare transire volebat ad Delphos, ubi oraculum Apollinis erat. Alcyone timebat, quia mare saepe periculosum erat.

But at one time, Ceyx had to sail. He wanted to cross the sea to Delphi, where the oracle of Apollo was. Alcyone was afraid because the sea was often dangerous.

Ceyx Alcyoni dixit, "Noli timere, mea cara. Tuto navigabo et cito revertar." Alcyone respondit, "Timeo, Ceyx. Te amittere nolo."

Ceyx said to Alcyone, "Do not be afraid, my dear. I will sail safely and return soon." Alcyone replied, "I am afraid, Ceyx. I do not want to lose you."

Ceyx navem paravit. Alcyone ad litus cum eo venit. Ceyx, "Vale, Alcyone. Amor meus tecum manet," dixit. Alcyone lacrimans, "Vale, Ceyx. Sis cautus," respondit.

Ceyx prepared the ship. Alcyone came with him to the shore. Ceyx said, "Farewell, Alcyone. My love remains with you." Alcyone, crying, replied, "Farewell, Ceyx. Be careful."

Ceyx in mare navigavit. Primo, mare tranquillum erat. Sed post paucos dies, tempestas horribilis coorta est. Venti fortes, undae magnae. Navigatio difficilis erat.

Ceyx sailed into the sea. At first, the sea was calm. But after a few days, a terrible storm arose. Strong winds, great waves. The sailing was difficult.

In palatio suo, Alcyone orabat pro Ceyce. Sed Ceyx in tempestate luctabatur. Nautae et Ceyx omnia faciebant ut navem servarent, sed frustra.

In her palace, Alcyone prayed for Ceyx. But Ceyx struggled in the storm. The sailors and Ceyx did everything to save the ship, but in vain.

Magna unda navem Ceycis cepit, et Ceyx in mare cecidit. Ceyx in undis clamavit, "Alcyone, te amo!" et in profundum demersus est.

A great wave seized Ceyx's ship, and Ceyx fell into the sea. In the waves, Ceyx cried out, "Alcyone, I love you!" and was swallowed by the depths.

Alcyone diu Ceycem exspectabat. Sed Ceyx non redibat. Tristis et sollicita erat.

Alcyone waited for Ceyx for a long time. But Ceyx did not return. She was sad and anxious.

Nocte quadam, in somnio, Ceyx Alcyoni apparuit. Ceyx dixit, "Alcyone, mea cara, peri in mare. Noli me amplius exspectare."

One night, in a dream, Ceyx appeared to Alcyone. Ceyx said, "Alcyone, my dear, I died in the sea. Do not wait for me any longer."

Alcyone expergefacta est et valde flevit. Ad litus cucurrit et in mare intuebatur. Tum, desperata, in aquas se iecit. "Ceyx, tecum esse volo," clamavit.

Alcyone woke up and wept greatly. She ran to the shore and looked out at the sea. Then, in despair, she threw herself into the water. "Ceyx, I want to be with you," she cried.

Dei, eorum amore commoti, mirum quiddam fecerunt. Ceyx et Alcyone in aves mutati sunt. In halcyones (alcedines) facti sunt, aves maritimae pulchrae.

The gods, moved by their love, performed a miracle. Ceyx and Alcyone were transformed into birds. They became kingfishers (halcyons), beautiful sea birds.

Halcyones in mare volabant, semper una. Ceyx et Alcyone, etiam in avium formis, amorem suum servabant.

The kingfishers flew over the sea, always together. Even in bird form, Ceyx and Alcyone kept their love.

Ita, cum tempestas est, halcyones in tranquillitate maris nidificare possunt. Hoc est tempus quod 'dies halcyonii' appellatur, dies tranquilli in medio hiemis.

Thus, when there is a storm, kingfishers can nest in the calm of the sea. This is the time called the 'halcyon days,' peaceful days in the middle of winter.

Ceyx and Alcyone, in bird form, always flew together, providing a beautiful example of love. People who watched them thought of eternal love and fidelity.

De Daedalo et Icaro

Daedalus, architectus et artifex peritus, cum filio Icaro in insula Creta habitabat.

Daedalus, a skilled architect and craftsman, lived with his son Icarus on the island of Crete.

Daedalus a rege Minos captus erat. Ei libertas cara erat, sed fugere difficile videbatur.

Daedalus had been captured by King Minos. Freedom was dear to him, but escaping seemed difficult.

Daedalus semper de libertate cogitabat. Die quodam, idea nova in mente eius venit. Aves in caelo vidit et dixit, "Si aves volare possunt, nos quoque possumus."

Daedalus always thought of freedom. One day, a new idea came to his mind. He saw birds in the sky and said, "If birds can fly, we can too."

Icarus, filius eius, iuvenis audax et curiosus, ad patrem venit et, "Quid facis, pater?" rogavit. Daedalus respondit, "Alas construimus. Nobis fugiendi via est."

Icarus, his son, a bold and curious youth, came to his father and asked, "What are you doing, father?" Daedalus replied, "We are building wings. This is our way to escape."

Daedalus alas ex pennis et cera fecit. Operam dedit ut alae firmas et leves essent. Icarus spectabat et mirabatur. "Mirabile!" exclamavit.

Daedalus made wings from feathers and wax. He worked carefully to make the wings strong and light. Icarus watched in amazement. "Incredible!" he exclaimed.

Cum alae paratae essent, Daedalus Icaro dixit, "Audi, Icare, moneo te. Ne nimis alto voles. Sol cerae nocebit."

When the wings were ready, Daedalus said to Icarus, "Listen, Icarus, I warn you. Do not fly too high. The sun will harm the wax."

Icarus, "Intellego, pater," respondit. Alas induerunt et parati ad volandum erant. Daedalus, "Parati sumus. Sequere me," dixit.

Icarus replied, "I understand, father." They put on the wings and were ready to fly. Daedalus said, "We are ready. Follow me."

Primum, volare difficile erat, sed mox facilius fiebat. Daedalus et Icarus super mare et terras volabant. Icarus gaudium magnum sentiebat. Libertas!

At first, flying was difficult, but soon it became easier. Daedalus and Icarus flew over the sea and land. Icarus felt great joy. Freedom!

Sed Icarus monitionem patris oblitus est. Altius et altius volabat. Daedalus clamavit, "Icare, descende! Periculosum est!" Sed Icarus non audivit.

But Icarus forgot his father's warning. He flew higher and higher. Daedalus shouted, "Icarus, come down! It's dangerous!" But Icarus did not listen.

Prope solem volavit. Sol calidus erat. Cera in alis eius coepit liquescere. Icarus sentiebat alas graves fieri.

He flew close to the sun. The sun was hot. The wax in his wings began to melt. Icarus felt the wings become heavy.

Icarus, territus, clamavit, "Pater, adiuva me!" Daedalus respexit et vidit Icarum cadere. "Icare!" exclamavit.

Terrified, Icarus cried out, "Father, help me!" Daedalus looked back and saw Icarus falling. "Icarus!" he exclaimed.

Icarus in mare cecidit. Daedalus ad locum ubi Icarus cecidit volavit, sed sero erat. Icarus in aqua mortuus erat.

Icarus fell into the sea. Daedalus flew to the place where Icarus had fallen, but it was too late. Icarus was dead in the water.

Daedalus flevit. Filius eius mortuus erat. In litore sedit et dixit, "Mea culpa, mea maxima culpa."

Daedalus wept. His son was dead. He sat on the shore and said, "It is my fault, my greatest fault."

Daedalus postea in Sicilia habitavit. Semper de Icaro cogitabat. Daedalus multas res creavit, sed numquam Icarum oblitus est.

Later, Daedalus lived in Sicily. He always thought of Icarus. Daedalus created many things, but he never forgot Icarus.

Homines de Daedalo et Icaro narrabant. "Videte Daedalum et Icarum. Sunt exempla audaciae et cautionis."

People told the story of Daedalus and Icarus. "Look at Daedalus and Icarus. They are examples of bravery and caution."

Icarus audax fuit, sed non satis cautus. Daedalus sapiens fuit, sed tristis propter filium. Eorum historia semper in memoria hominum manebit.

Icarus was brave, but not cautious enough. Daedalus was wise, but sad because of his son. Their story will always remain in people's memory.

Ita, Daedalus et Icarus in fabulis et in historiis manserunt. Exemplum amoris patris et audaciae filii. Monitio de periculis superbiae et inobedientiae.

Thus, Daedalus and Icarus remained in stories and legends. An example of a father's love and a son's courage. A warning about the dangers of pride and disobedience.

De Aesone Restituto

In antiqua Graecia, Medea, mulier magicae artis perita, vivebat.

In ancient Greece, Medea, a woman skilled in the magical arts, lived.

Jason, Argonautarum dux, eam amabat. Aeson, Jasonis pater, senex et infirmus erat.

Jason, the leader of the Argonauts, loved her. Aeson, Jason's father, was old and frail.

Jason ad Medeam venit et dixit, "Medea, mea cara, pater meus, Aeson, senex est. Potestne tua magica arte iuventutem ei reddere?"

Jason came to Medea and said, "Medea, my dear, my father, Aeson, is old. Can your magical art restore his youth?"

Medea, "Possibile est," respondit. "Sed opus magnum et difficile est. Tamen, pro te, conabor."

Medea replied, "It is possible. But it is a great and difficult task. However, for you, I will try."

Medea in silvam ivit ut herbas magicas colligeret. Multas noctes et dies in silva mansit. Herbas, gemmas, et aquam ex fonte magico collegit.

Medea went into the forest to gather magical herbs. She stayed in the forest for many nights and days. She collected herbs, gems, and water from a magical spring.

Cum omnia parata essent, Medea ad Aesonem ivit. Aeson in lecto iacebat, debilis et senex. Medea, "Aesone, te iuvenem faciam," dixit.

When everything was ready, Medea went to Aeson. Aeson was lying in bed, weak and old. Medea said, "Aeson, I will make you young."

Medea caldarium magnum fieri praecepit. Aqua et herbae in caldario posita sunt. Medea carmina magica cantavit et circulos magicos fecit.

Medea ordered a large cauldron to be made. Water and herbs were placed in the cauldron. Medea sang magical chants and drew magical circles.

Aeson, "Quid facis, Medea?" rogavit. Medea, "Artem magicam. Tace et exspecta," respondit.

Aeson asked, "What are you doing, Medea?" Medea replied, "Magic. Be silent and wait."

Medea herbas in aquam misit. Caldarium luce et fumo implevit. Omnes qui aderant mirabantur.

Medea threw the herbs into the water. The cauldron filled with light and smoke. Everyone present was amazed.

Post multas horas, Medea, "Aesone, in aquam veni," dixit. Aeson in aquam lente descendit. Sentiebat se mutare.

After many hours, Medea said, "Aeson, come into the water." Aeson slowly stepped into the water. He felt himself changing.

Aeson in aqua diu mansit. Cum ex aqua ascendit, mirum! Aeson iuvenis erat! Capilli eius nigri, corpus eius firmum. Aeson et omnes qui aderant stupebant.

Aeson stayed in the water for a long time. When he rose from the water, it was a miracle! Aeson was young! His hair was black, his body strong. Aeson and everyone present were astonished.

Aeson ad speculum ivit et se spectavit. "Incredibile!" exclamavit. "Medea, gratias tibi ago! Me iuvenem fecisti!"

Aeson went to the mirror and looked at himself. "Incredible!" he exclaimed. "Medea, thank you! You made me young!"

Jason ad patrem venit et, "Pater, te vix recognosco! Medea, mirabilis es!" dixit. Medea risit et, "Magica ars potens est," respondit.

Jason came to his father and said, "Father, I hardly recognize you! Medea, you are amazing!" Medea laughed and replied, "Magic is powerful."

Aeson, iuvenis factus, multos annos postea vixit. Fuit sicut iuvenis alius, fortis et vivax.

Aeson, now made young, lived for many years afterward. He was like any other young man, strong and lively.

Homines de Medea et eius arte magica narrabant. "Videte Medeam, mulierem magicam, quae Aesonem iuvenem fecit!"

People spoke of Medea and her magical art. "Look at Medea, the magical woman, who made Aeson young!"

Medea et Jason felices erant. Medea arte sua alia mirabilia fecit. Sed semper meminerunt diei cum Aeson iuvenis factus est.

Medea and Jason were happy. Medea performed other wonders with her magic. But they always remembered the day when Aeson was made young.

Ita, in fabulis et in historiis, Medea celebratur ut mulier magicae artis potentissima. Exemplum artis magicae et potentiae amoris.

Thus, in stories and legends, Medea is celebrated as a woman of the most powerful magical art. An example of magical skill and the power of love.

De Hermaphrodito et Salmacis

Hermaphroditus, filius Hermis et Aphroditae, puer pulcher et fortis, iter longum faciebat.

Hermaphroditus, the son of Hermes and Aphrodite, a beautiful and strong boy, was on a long journey.

Multas terras et insulas videbat.

He saw many lands and islands.

In quadam insula, Salmacis, nympha pulchra, in suo fonte habitabat. Salmacis aquas et silvas amabat. Erat nympha laeta et libera.

187

On a certain island, Salmacis, a beautiful nymph, lived in her fountain. Salmacis loved the waters and forests. She was a happy and free nymph.

Die quodam, Hermaphroditus ad fontem Salmacis venit. Sitim habebat et aquam puram bibere volebat. Salmacis eum vidit et statim eum amavit.

One day, Hermaphroditus came to Salmacis' fountain. He was thirsty and wanted to drink pure water. Salmacis saw him and immediately loved him.

Salmacis ad Hermaphroditum accessit et dixit, "Salve, puer pulcher. Quis es?" Hermaphroditus respondit, "Ego sum Hermaphroditus, filius Hermis et Aphroditae. Et tu?"

Salmacis approached Hermaphroditus and said, "Hello, handsome boy. Who are you?" Hermaphroditus replied, "I am Hermaphroditus, the son of Hermes and Aphrodite. And you?"

"Ego sum Salmacis, nympha huius fontis. Hic locus pulcher est. Vis hic manere?" Salmacis rogavit. Hermaphroditus, "Non possum. Iter longum habeo," respondit.

"I am Salmacis, the nymph of this fountain. This place is beautiful. Do you want to stay here?" Salmacis asked. Hermaphroditus replied, "I cannot. I have a long journey."

Salmacis, "Mane paulum. Aquae meae dulces et frigidae sunt. Te delectabunt," dixit. Hermaphroditus acquievit et in fonte natavit.

Salmacis said, "Stay a little while. My waters are sweet and cold. They will delight you." Hermaphroditus agreed and swam in the fountain.

Salmacis Hermaphroditum spectabat et magis magisque eum amabat. "Hermaphrodite, tecum esse cupio," clamavit.

Salmacis watched Hermaphroditus and loved him more and more. "Hermaphroditus, I wish to be with you," she cried.

Hermaphroditus e fonte exiit et, "Ego iter meum pergere debeo," dixit. Salmacis tristis erat. "Ne abeas, te precor," rogavit.

Hermaphroditus left the fountain and said, "I must continue my journey." Salmacis was sad. "Do not leave, I beg you," she pleaded.

Salmacis deos oravit ut cum Hermaphrodito semper esset. Dei preces eius audierunt. Mirum! Hermaphroditus et Salmacis in unum corpus coniuncti sunt!

Salmacis prayed to the gods to always be with Hermaphroditus. The gods heard her prayers. Miraculously! Hermaphroditus and Salmacis were merged into one body!

Hermaphroditus et Salmacis unum facti sunt, corpus et anima. Corpus eorum erat et masculinum et femininum. Hermaphroditus stupuit et, "Quid hoc est?" clamavit.

Hermaphroditus and Salmacis became one, body and soul. Their body was both male and female. Hermaphroditus was astonished and cried, "What is this?"

Salmacis, in eodem corpore, "Nunc semper una sumus, Hermaphrodite. Amor noster aeternus est," dixit.

Salmacis, in the same body, said, "Now we are always together, Hermaphroditus. Our love is eternal."

Hermaphroditus tristis erat. Libertatem suam amiserat. Sed Salmacis laeta erat, quia amorem suum tenebat.

Hermaphroditus was sad. He had lost his freedom. But Salmacis was happy, because she had her love.

Hermaphroditus et Salmacis in illo loco manserunt. Corpus eorum novum erat, sed animae separatae manebant.

Hermaphroditus and Salmacis stayed in that place. Their body was new, but their souls remained separate.

Homines de Hermaphrodito et Salmacide narrabant. "Videte Hermaphroditum et Salmacidem. Sunt exempla amoris et mutationis."

People spoke of Hermaphroditus and Salmacis. "Look at Hermaphroditus and Salmacis. They are examples of love and transformation."

Ita, in fabulis et historiis, Hermaphroditus et Salmacis manserunt. Exemplum amoris potens, sed etiam monitio de desideriis nimis magnis.

Thus, in stories and histories, Hermaphroditus and Salmacis remained. An example of powerful love, but also a warning about desires that are too great.

Hermaphroditus et Salmacis in aqua fontis vixerunt. Eorum historia multis narrata est, de amore, de transformatione, et de natura duali.

Hermaphroditus and Salmacis lived in the water of the fountain. Their story was told by many, about love, transformation, and dual nature.

Lingua Latina

111 Interlinear

Latin – English Conversations

More books

More ressources

Endorsements by leading Latinists

All on discoverlatin.com